Eat Like a Local

LONDON

BLOOMSBURY PUBLISHING
LONDON · OXFORD · NEW YORK · NEW DELHI · SYDNEY

Welcome to London

There's never been a better time to eat or drink like a Londoner. New restaurants and drinking establishments open here every week, constantly upping the base level and increasing the options on offer. The dining scene, in particular, is booming: where once eating out meant a starched world of fine dining accessible only to a few, now more people than ever, across generations and income brackets, eat out regularly – in noodle bars, at street food markets, sushi counters, steak restaurants, pie shops and Michelin-starred restaurants.

As home cooks and food shoppers, Londoners have become a lot more discerning (and spoilt). Farmers' markets sprout and bear fruit in most neighbourhoods. The city boasts numerous sourdough bakeries, coffee roasters, craft brewers, picklers, charcutiers and cheese makers. And there are multiple quality delicatessens, cafés and independent bottle shops, each proactively seeking to stock and promote locally made products, while also providing consumers with access to the very best from elsewhere across the country and beyond.

Few, if any, of London's best restaurants are secret or hidden, though you do need to seek, ask and be willing to venture beyond the obvious chains that appear on every high street. An open mind will be rewarded by a city whose kitchen has something for everybody. Indeed, this cosmopolitan capital's palate is evidently multicultural – you can travel the world on the back of an Oyster card, while also feasting on food that's very definitely British.

Explore the City

Central Bustling **Soho** is the epicentre of casual, concept dining. Busy from early afternoon to the end of the night, all tastes are catered for, though expect queues as few restaurants take reservations. Nearby **Chinatown** has a similar vibe, whereas dining in **Covent Garden**, **Holborn** and **Fitzrovia** is marginally more relaxed, with a mix of large name chains, long-established independents and bookable bistros.

North Central Formerly a no-go area, **King's Cross** is now a near-fully regenerated zone with multiple enticing concepts attracting a mix of office workers, commuters and local residents. Nearby **Clerkenwell** and **Islington** attract a similar clientele, thanks to bijou clusters of characterful, mid-range and informal restaurants.

South Central Perennially busy chain restaurants line the **Southbank**, attracting tourists, theatre buffs and museum-goers. Local young professionals tend to swarm to areas slightly beyond the waterfront, such as the charming and foodie-oriented **Bermondsey** to the east of **London Bridge**, and the vibrant edges of **Borough Market**.

The City & Shoreditch **City** workers are well-fed in high-end restaurants and by fast-paced lunch concepts. In the evenings, suits mix with (or change into) creatives on the eastern edge of the Square Mile; **Shoreditch**, **Hoxton** and **Old Street** are home to some of London's most cutting-edge restaurants and bars.

East Londoners used to head to **Kingsland Road** for authentic Vietnamese, and to **Dalston** and **Stoke Newington** for great value Turkish feasts... and they still do. But fashionable **Hackney** is perhaps now better known for its youthful creatives, forward-thinking neighbourhood restaurants, artisan bakeries, coffee shops and breweries with tap-rooms.

West End High-end restaurants, classic hotel bars and a taste of the good life are de rigueur in **Mayfair**, **St James's** and the western end of **Piccadilly**, where both dining and diners are smart, mature, refined and well-funded. There's a slightly more relaxed, continental feel to **Marylebone**, though restaurants and cafés remain classy.

West Elegant wine bars, smart pub kitchens, safe mini-chains and modern juice bars serve the well-heeled residents of **Kensington** and **Chelsea**, not least in the once cutting-edge, now more rounded, **Notting Hill**. There are a scattering of top-end and chichi places too, particularly in and around the hotels and department stores of **Belgravia** and **Knightsbridge**.

South Though some lament recent gentrification, south London retains an edge and an air of independence. Locals are rightly proud of their mix of ethnic cuisine and contemporary neighbourhood restaurants. The likes of **Brixton** and **Peckham** attract young eaters and restaurateurs, and there are long-established local gems in **Camberwell**, **Clapham** and **Stockwell**.

North Affluent northern neighbourhoods of **St John's Wood**, **Primrose Hill**, **Hampstead** and **Highgate** feature village-like high streets with reliable, if uninspiring, chains and bars. Their backstreets, on the other hand, contain some of London's best pubs and gastropubs – ideal retreats post park walk or urban meander.

Meet the Locals

Ed Smith

rocketandsquash.com

The author of the website rocketandsquash.com, a food journal regularly updated with restaurant reviews, recipes, news round-ups and short films, Ed has featured as a resident chef for the *Guardian*'s supplement *Cook* and guest cookery writer at the *Independent on Sunday*. His debut cookbook, *On the Side*, was shortlisted for the inaugural Jane Grigson Trust Award.

Catherine & Gavin Hanly

hot-dinners.com

Co-founders of Hot Dinners, an eating out website for London that was set up in 2009 as an alternative to directory restaurant sites, Catherine and Gavin bring a new way of looking at the London restaurant scene and cover everything from pop-ups to openings. They were first listed in the *Evening Standard*'s 1000 most influential Londoners list in 2012 and, with the exception of 2014, have been on the list every year since.

Celia Brooks

celiabrooks.com

A former private chef for director Stanley Kubrick and author of nine cookbooks, including her latest: *SuperVeg*. She makes regular television appearances and runs a London food tour business called Gastrotours. She is the only person licensed by Borough Market to run tours there, and writes regularly for their website.

Chloe Sachdev

unseen247.com

Specialising in food, drink and travel trends, Chloe is a freelance writer who contributes to various publications including *Condé Nast Traveller*, *Gourmet Traveller* and the *Evening Standard*. She is the co-founder of lifestyle and culture newsletter *Unseen 24/7*.

George Reynolds

egoscriptor.space

George Reynolds is still clinging onto a 2016 food writing award (for pieces completed in 2015), which he has parlayed into occasional work at *The Sunday Times*, *Noble Rot* and Eater London.

Rosie Birkett

rosiebirkett.com

A food writer, food stylist and author based in Hackney, east London. Rosie has written two books: *A Lot On Her Plate* and, most recently, *East London Food* – a book exploring the rich and diverse culinary culture of her London neighbourhood.

Liz & Max Haarala Hamilton

haaralahamilton.com

A photographic duo specialising in capturing food, people and places. As well as photographing cookbooks they shoot the weekly Food and Drinks pages for the *Telegraph*, *Stella* and *Grazia*, and are regular contributors to numerous magazines, including *Boat*, *Huck*, *OFM* and *Voyeur*.

Joanne Gould

joeatslondon.com

A freelance food writer who has contributed to publications such as *Cosmopolitan*, and websites Londonist and The Pool. She is also the author of joeatslondon.com, a London-based blog filled with recipes and reviews.

Kar-Shing Tong

@ks_ate_here

A native New Zealander who has been eating his way through London for the last decade, documenting each dish along the way. He shares his experiences and culinary journey around the world through Instagram and Twitter, and has been recognised as one of London's top food influencers.

Sharlene Carpenter

essor.co.uk

Born and raised in London and indebted to her mother's traditional British home cooking, Sharlene shares her love of food as a guide for Secret Food Tours, where she gives exemplary information to visitors on the ins and outs of English food and its history.

Victoria Stewart

victoria-stewart.com

A food and travel journalist who, before going freelance and writing for national newspapers and magazines, used to be the food editor at the *Evening Standard*. She's also the creator of the blog londonstreetfoodie. co.uk, which she began in 2012.

BREAKFAST

A true Londoner eats a hastily spread slice of toast while running for the bus, or grabs a yoghurt and granola pot, or a ham and cheese croissant at the same time as they pick up a coffee to go. But these habits are probably not the best ones to follow. Not least because breakfast and brunch can provide an ideal opportunity for a relaxed and affordable meal out – and potentially the pinnacle of your eating that day. If you're lucky enough to stay in a hotel where breakfast is cooked to order, stay put and order a plate of thick-sliced back bacon, free-range pork sausages, black pudding, sautéed mushrooms and eggs done the way you like.

If you plan to venture beyond the roof you slept under, you'll need to formulate a plan, rather than take a punt. For a nation so well known for its "Full English", it is surprisingly difficult to find a London breakfast worth getting out of bed for (let alone getting on the tube).

You have two options: the classic London breakfast plus continental pastries; or contemporary, international-style brunching. In the former category there's everything from the glitz, glamour and clatter of The Wolseley (page 17), where the finest *Viennoiserie* are offered alongside kippers, superlative omelette Arnold Bennett and everything in between; through devilled kidneys on toast and first-class bacon sandwiches at places like St John Bread and Wine (opposite); all the way to a greasy spoonful of old England at a local "caff". London's cosmopolitan make-up comes to the fore in the second category, as Australasian-influenced restaurants show us how avocado on toast should be done; and restaurants representing truly global cuisine offer game-changing ways to start your day.

See also Dishoom (page 56), Silva's (page 22)

① St John Bread and Wine

Recommended by Ed Smith

"This is my first choice for a proper English breakfast – which doesn't actually mean a full fry-up. Think, instead, of THE benchmark bacon sandwich, grilled kippers or even devilled kidneys on toast. There's something particularly restorative about the austere room too; perhaps the lack of clutter and distraction just helps to get the day off in the right direction"—*ES*

94–96 Commercial Street, Spitalfields E1 6LZ
stjohngroup.uk.com • +44 2072510848
Open 7 days • ££££

② Granger & Co.

Recommended by Joanne Gould

"I love the pink, marble and gold decor. Lovely Australian breakfasts, usually a bit healthier than most. You can sit outside if you're early enough to bag a spot. The ricotta hot cakes are amazing, as are the sweetcorn fritters"—*JG*

7 Pancras Square, King's Cross N1C 4AG
(see website for other locations)
grangerandco.com • +44 2030582567
Open 7 days • ££££

③ Hawksmoor

Recommended by Joanne Gould, Kar-Shing Tong

"It's my go-to place for breakfast and you only need to take one look at the Breakfast for Two to understand why: a cast-iron dish filled to the brim with sausages, bacon chop, black pudding, eggs and other delectable items. It could easily be a breakfast for four and it certainly makes the offer of unlimited toast seem wholly redundant"—*KST*

11 Langley Street, Covent Garden WC2H 9JG
(see website for other locations)
thehawksmoor.com • +44 2074209390
Open 7 days • ££££

④ The Wolseley

Recommended by Ed Smith

'Less a restaurant, more an institution. The Wolseley is set up like a grand European café. While it's open from early until very late, the combination of food grazing and people watching is most inviting at breakfast. An extensive menu includes first class *Viennoiserie*, Bircher mueslis and so on, but I'm almost always drawn to the omelette Arnold Bennett"—*ES*

160 Piccadilly, St James's W1J 9EB
thewolseley.com • +44 2074996996
Open 7 days • ££££

⑤ Royal China Club

Recommended by George Reynolds

"My favourite food ritual in London is a leisurely late brunch at Royal China Club, the Baker Street institution (aka the one you can book). It starts with wave after wave of impeccable, beautiful dim sum, and finishes about an hour later with a whole crispy duck and wok-charred noodles. You will drink a lot of jasmine tea. You will not require dinner" —*GR*

40–42 Baker Street, Marylebone W1U 7AJ
(see website for other locations)
theroyalchina.co.uk • +44 2074863898
Open 7 days • ££££

6 Duck and Waffle

Recommended by Catherine & Gavin Hanly

"The weekend breakfast here is the best in town (and a total bargain given the location at the top of Heron Tower). The views over London are spectacular and you can try their iconic, namesake dish alongside more breakfasty offerings like Colombian eggs or ox cheek Benedict"—*C&GH*

110 Bishopsgate, The City EC2N 4AY
duckandwaffle.com • +44 2036407310
Open 24/7 • ££££

. . . .

7 Café Z Bar

Recommended by Rosie Birkett

"I love it for the mixed *menemen* – a Turkish egg dish with spicy Turkish sausage and onion that comes served on a sizzling hot metal plate and really hits the spot (particularly when hungover)"—*RB*

58 Stoke Newington High Street, Stoke Newington N16 7PB
+44 2072757523
Open 7 days • ££££

CLASSIC LONDON

Studies of historic London recall restaurants influenced by French fine dining, with grand rooms and silvered place settings. But those places were for the few. In fact this metropolis was built on the back of chophouses, pie and mash and fish and chip shops, salt beef beigel bakeries and "greasy spoon" cafés. Though less prevalent now, these places still exist, with fish and chips still particularly popular; locals standing in line for their portion of battered haddock and cod, chips fried in beef dripping and doused with vinegar, and maybe a pickle on the side.

The pie shops – serving eel pie, mashed potato and parsley liquor – are easily identifiable by their uniform decor: gold lettering on green or brown backboards, and green and cream tiles both inside and out. These informal eateries are often found on or near the traditional working-class market streets, such as Broadway Market in east London, Chapel Market in Islington, East Street Market off the Walworth Road in south London, and all over Whitechapel and Bethnal Green. A clutch of timeless London greasy spoons continues, too, replete with unintentionally trendy tiles on the walls, Formica-topped tables and a hint of cigarette ingrained in the floor. These "caffs" serve huge, appetite busting, all day breakfasts: fried eggs, hash browns, fried bread, large puddles of baked beans, milky builder's tea, and probably something else fried to go with it.

The Classics have seen new cuisines and trends come and go; yet they remain, pleasingly, knowingly, unchanged. It's worth seeking them out for a gratifying fried or mashed snapshot of real London.

⑧ Sweetings

Recommended by Ed Smith

"A clear forerunner to St John (page 27) and a restaurant that's done a great deal to shape London's modern British menu. This is a lunch-only seafood restaurant on the edge of the City which, while full of pinstripes, braces and black credit cards, is also without buff and polish. There's more than a whiff of Old Billingsgate wholesale fish market about the place, with a menu that pits scampi and bacon against fillets of hake served with lobster-spiked mash; Welsh rarebit on toast versus turbot and white wine reduction sauce"—*ES*

39 Queen Victoria Street, The City EC4N 4SA
sweetingsrestaurant.co.uk • +44 2072483062
Open Monday to Friday • £££

⑨ Goddards at Greenwich

Recommended by Sharlene Carpenter

"Tantalising pie, mash and parsley liquor. It's been around since the 1890s and is a family-run business. The classics include the steak and kidney or steak and ale pie: the gravy spills out from the pastry crust onto the plate so you have a crunchy but soft texture with succulent meat that melts in your mouth"—SC

22 King William Walk, Greenwich SE10 9HU
goddardsatgreenwich.co.uk • +44 2083059612
Open 7 days • £££££

⑩ Maria's Market Café

Recommended by Kar-Shing Tong

"Located in the heart of Borough Market, you can dine on classic no-frills London favourites such as bubble and squeak while trains run over tracks above you"—KST

8 Southwark Street, Borough Market SE1 1TL
boroughmarket.org.uk • +44 2074071002
Open Wednesday to Saturday • £££££

⑪ Silva's

Recommended by Catherine & Gavin Hanly

"Our favourite greasy spoon. This Italian-run old-school café does excellent doorstop-bread toast in the mornings and their takeaway sandwiches are great. But mainly we come for the lovely staff"—C&GH

220 Shaftesbury Avenue, Bloomsbury WC2H 8DP
+44 2072400028
Closed Sunday • £££££

⑫ Beigel Bake

Recommended by George Reynolds, Victoria Stewart

"There is no doubt in my mind that the salt beef beigel here is, pound for pound, the best food in London. The meat is rich and really quite salty (funny, that), and the mustard on top will deviate your septum. But the real wonder is the beigel itself: soft, and pliable, but with just the right amount of bite and chew"—*GR*

159 Brick Lane, Shoreditch E1 6SB
+44 2077290616
Open 24/7 • £££££

⑬ Poppie's

Recommended by Joanne Gould, Victoria Stewart

"Feels authentically old-school, like the sort of place I'd go to with my grandparents as a child"—*JG*

An authentic London fish and chips restaurant, with one eye on a nostalgic, battered and newspaper-wrapped past, and the other firmly on providing quality, sustainably sourced fish for a contemporary market.

6–8 Hanbury Street, Spitalfields E1 6QR
(see website for other locations)
poppiesfishandchips.co.uk • +44 2072470892
Open 7 days • ££££

⑭ The Golden Hind

Recommended by Celia Brooks

"This classic, no-frills Greek-run chippie has been going for over 100 years.
While the neighbourhood around it has become exceedingly gentrified and
fancy, it remains honest and down to earth. Perfect golden battered haddock,
crispy chips and luscious mushy peas are a must (and portions are huge)"—*CB*

73 Marylebone Lane, Marylebone W1U 2PN
goldenhindrestaurant.com • +44 2074863644
Closed Sunday • £££

BRITISH

There's traditional British: three piece tweed suits, red cords, and the pride, pomp and circumstance of the Glorious Twelfth (of August – the first day of the grouse shooting season), all of which is fuelled by restaurants with starched white tablecloths and stiff upper lips. Think game birds, steak and kidney pie, fillets of venison and vats of red wine; and also of roast beef carved tableside, plus oysters, caviar, lobsters and champagne.

London certainly has restaurants for all those things: Rules (opposite) for the game and the pies and Simpson's in the Strand (page 30) for the carvery, for example. But there's also a definite Modern British genre now too – which incorporates the localism and foraging of New Nordic cuisine, the sleek aesthetic of Parisian bistronomy, and the insistence on using seasonal ingredients at their peak.

Perhaps most importantly, it is also rooted in the honest, nose-to-tail ethos of Fergus Henderson's St John (opposite). Disciples of this famous restaurant write their menus in proper nouns only, make thrifty and inventive use of all of the animals they buy in, making light of the once winced at offal, and take confidence in the knowledge that deceptively simple and flavour first is the way forward for their food. Unlike the Old School, the tables are uncovered and clattery, the front of house are your new, laconic (though still professional) mates, and an informal, accessible-to-all meal is utmost on everyone's agenda. Their Modern British food is among the very best dining you'll find in this city.

See also Noble Rot (page 98), The Quality Chop House (page 120), St John Bread and Wine (page 15), Sweetings (page 21)

⑮ St John Bar and Restaurant

Recommended by Joanne Gould, Ed Smith

"Not just the headquarters of Fergus Henderson's St John brand, this is the spiritual home of nose-to-tail eating and, to an extent, British food. Yes, there's bone marrow and offal, but there's also deceptively simply treated fish and vegetables; it's honest cooking. I like it as much for a quick, solo rarebit on toast and cider in the bar, as I do a full-on, celebratory suckling pig roast with friends"—*ES*

"The ultimate nose-to-tail eating in unfussy, stark surroundings"—*JG*

26 St John Street, Clerkenwell EC1M 4AY
stjohngroup.uk.com • +44 2072510848
Open 7 days • £££££

⑯ Rules

Recommended by Ed Smith

"Rules is, apparently, London's oldest restaurant (1798), and it plays up to that title, with red velvet banquets, starched white tablecloths, and hundreds of pictures capturing its Covent Garden theatreland heritage. There are always oysters, pies, and steak and kidney suet puddings, plus classics like sticky toffee, fruit crumbles and English cheeses. For me, though, the time to go is September through February, when much of the menu is game-focused (pheasant, partridge, hare, venison). Nothing fussy or over the top, just British"—*ES*

35 Maiden Lane, Covent Garden WC2E 7LB
rules.co.uk • +44 2078365314
Open 7 days • £££££

17 Holborn Dining Room

Recommended by Rosie Birkett, Kar-Shing Tong

"Holborn Dining Room embodies the very best of British cuisine. Ingredients are the finest that Britain has to offer and the food is expertly prepared by one of Britain's most talented chefs, Calum Franklin, who is single-handedly making the humble beef Wellington and pork pie cool again"—*KST*

"I love the Holborn Dining Room at the Rosewood where chef Calum Franklin excels in making pies. His intricate pork pies not only look incredible, but are the real deal to eat, with perfectly moist meat and delicate jelly"—*RB*

252 High Holborn, Holborn WC1V 7EN
holborndiningroom.com • +44 2037478633
Open 7 days • ££££

18 Simpson's in the Strand

Recommended by Ed Smith

"Recently refurbished, this buffed yet old-school dining room feels as grand, classy and ostentatiously English as you'd expect for a restaurant attached to the Savoy Hotel. Although there's a contemporary touch to much of the food menu, I love the opulent carving trolleys that circulate all day, every day serving pink roast beef, lamb and all the trimmings"—*ES*

100 Strand, Covent Garden WC2R 0EW
simpsonsinthestrand.co.uk • +44 2074202111
Open 7 days • ££££

19 The Clove Club

Recommended by Catherine & Gavin Hanly

"The Clove Club is a brilliant example of how dynamic and exciting the London restaurant scene is right now. We've seen chefs Isaac, Daniel and Johnny come up through the supper club ranks to their current exalted status as the highest British restaurant on the World's 50 Best Restaurants list. If time or money prevent you from trying the tasting menu, you can still get a flavour of the food by working your way through the bar menu"—*C&GH*

380 Old Street, Shoreditch EC1V 9LT
thecloveclub.com • +44 2077296496
Closed Sunday • ££££

20 Clipstone

Recommended by Ed Smith

"Clipstone does everything right: the setting is informal and relaxed – open kitchen, ferments on the windowsills and cosy, convivial seating; the drinks are impeccably chosen, with quality, accessible wines on tap as well as interesting drops by the bottle; and the food is rooted in seasonal ingredients, artfully matched, and cooked without style ever exceeding substance. The influences are global but that's very much indicative of modern British cooking"—*ES*

5 Clipstone Street, Fitzrovia W1W 6BB
clipstonerestaurant.co.uk • +44 2076370871
Closed Sunday • ££££

㉑ Elliot's

Recommended by Chloe Sachdev

"Great for modern European fare. Their menu of sharing plates – think Parisian
neo bistro meets modern British – is delicious and affordable. It also has one
of the best wine lists in London"—*CS*

12 Stoney Street, Borough Market SE1 9AD
elliotscafe.com • +44 2074037436
Closed Sunday • ££££

㉒ Lyle's

*Recommended by Rosie Birkett,
Ed Smith, Victoria Stewart*

"Lyle's in Shoreditch serves some
of the most exceptional and
delicious British cuisine out there
at the moment. Chef James Lowe
is unrelenting in sourcing the very
best British ingredients. He used
to be head chef at St John Bread
and Wine (page 15), so his approach
is seemingly straightforward but
there is a lot of care and thought
that goes on behind the scenes. It
comes through in the food, which
is always beautifully well balanced,
interesting, and above all, absolutely
delicious. It's particularly good to eat
there during game season as Lowe is
really passionate about celebrating
game, something he considers to be
one of Britain's strongest culinary
offerings"—*RB*

*56 Shoreditch High Street,
Shoreditch E1 6JJ
lyleslondon.com • +44 2030115911
Closed Sunday • £££££*

PUB KITCHEN

Until the early 1990s, you wouldn't go to the local drinking hole and expect an enjoyable feed. Now, though, pubs with good kitchens (the so-called gastropubs) are ten a penny, and often the first port of call when Londoners are considering a relaxed meal out. A few are in the very centre of town, but most tend to be in more residential areas or near the parks, making them reliable, convivial, neighbourhood favourites.

Gastropubs are accessible, affordable and unpretentious. You can still lean against the bar and have a pint, perhaps with a warm Scotch egg or house-made sausage roll. But you are also able to sit down for a restaurant-quality meal. Some have full table service, others keep things more casual and require you to place your food order at the same time you're buying a round of drinks.

There'll almost always be fish and chips and a burger on the menu, probably a pie or steak and hand-cut chips too. The best, however, tend to offer a bit more than that. Their menus will change daily, follow a seasonal theme, and champion British farmers and producers. Picture terrines and warm salads; a catch-of-the-day fish with piquant greens or punchy broth; prime cuts of meat with innovative sides; and crowd-pleasing desserts like sticky toffee pudding, custard tart and panna cotta served with elan, a little twist, or both. All of this within the welcoming setting of a pub, where the tap beer selection is considered, and wine list discerning but not too pricey.

See also SUNDAY ROAST (page 38)

23 The Eagle

Recommended by Liz & Max Haarala Hamilton

"It's the original gastrobar and the food is still amazing!" —*L&MHH*

Though from the outside this Clerkenwell pub looks unassuming, it's credited as the genesis of Britain's gastropub movement – the first place to serve both excellent, contemporary food and pints of beer in informal surroundings. Many of the best places spawned directly from this kitchen, and hundreds of others have copied the format.

159 Farringdon Road, Clerkenwell EC1R 3AL
theeaglefarringdon.co.uk • +44 2078371353
Open 7 days • ££££

24 The Canton Arms

Recommended by Liz & Max Haarala Hamilton

"Our favourite and our local where you can go for an amazing meal or just to have one of their toasties. The chefs there are always changing the menu to match what's in season, so you never know what you are going to get" —*L&MHH*

177 South Lambeth Road, Stockwell SW8 1XP
cantonarms.com • +44 2075828710
Open 7 days • ££££

25 The Camberwell Arms

Recommended by Liz & Max Haarala Hamilton

"Their roasts are brilliant. Rotisserie chicken and their house hot-smoked salmon is what takes us back there!" —*L&MHH*

65 Camberwell Church Street, Camberwell SE5 8TR
thecamberwellarms.co.uk • +44 2073584364
Open 7 days • ££££

26 The Drapers Arms

Recommended by George Reynolds, Kar-Shing Tong

"Like the thick slabs of bread with good salty old-school butter plunked on your table here without ceremony, lunch or dinner at The Drapers Arms is not always the most finessed. But – particularly in winter – its gutsiness is sometimes the ideal tonic to food that has been dressed up into anonymity: soup, that most unfashionable of dishes, is a panacea on a cold day; pies are huge ribsticking affairs that leave you utterly contented. Come hungry"—*GR*

44 Barnsbury Street, Islington N1 1ER
thedrapersarms.com • +44 2076190348
Open 7 days • ££££

㉗ Marksman

Recommended by Rosie Birkett, Chloe Sachdev, Ed Smith

"Fantastic British pub food with two former St John (page 27) chefs at the helm. I adore their chicken pie with buttery homemade pastry and a stock-rich sauce flecked with tarragon"—*RB*

"A typical London boozer that was also crowned Michelin Pub of the Year. It's no wonder with dishes such as snails cured with Tamworth peas and lovage, devilled cuttlefish, and addictive beef and barley buns"—*CS*

254 Hackney Road, Shoreditch E2 7SJ
marksmanpublichouse.com • +44 2077397393
Open 7 days • ££££

SUNDAY ROAST

A Sunday roast is both a meal and an event. On the food side, it's blushing pink slices of roast beef or lamb, unctuous pork topped with crunchy crackling, or juicy chicken with golden skin. Next to the meat will be roast potatoes with crisp edges and fluffy interiors, a few seasonal vegetables and litres of gravy. There are other tweaks and twists (Yorkshire puddings with beef, mint sauce with lamb, herby stuffing with chicken, and so on), but ultimately it's a tried, tested and much-loved formula.

Yet, a Sunday roast also means a gathering of friends or family. For many Londoners, this is the most sociable meal of the week. "Do you fancy meeting for a roast?" is code for catching up on recent endeavours, celebrating significant events or misdemeanours, and putting the end of weekend blues on hold for as long as possible. Many restaurants serve whole roast joints to share, rather than portioned plates, echoing the familial nature of this moment. Inevitably, the pint glasses and wine bottles stack up.

The informality and conviviality makes the meal ideally suited to pub kitchens (page 34); you'll struggle to find a gastropub that doesn't serve a roast on a Sunday. Very few will have any food left beyond 3pm (if their kitchen is open at all), and those with the best reputation get booked out weeks in advance (particularly from autumn through to spring) so don't delay.

See also PUB KITCHEN (page 34), The Quality Chop House (page 120)

28 Blacklock

Recommended by Kar-Shing Tong

"The Sunday roast here is a celebration of one of Britain's greatest traditions. With a drinks menu to match, this is where Sundays are made"—*KST*

Blacklock serves great value roasts, as well as quality chops and steaks grilled over fire, lubricated by classic cocktails and to the soundtrack of upbeat tunes. Its basement sites are popular, vibrant and always fun.

24 Great Windmill Street, Soho W1D 7LG
(see website for other locations)
theblacklock.com • +44 2034416996
Open 7 days • ££££

29 The Windsor Castle

Recommended by Rosie Birkett

"The Windsor on Lower Clapton Road has a relaxed vibe, a broad selection of craft beer and does a good hearty Sunday roast. You can easily while away a lazy Sunday afternoon there; it's also ideally located for popping into P. Franco (page 96) for a glass of something really memorable and some more food if you get peckish"—*RB*

135 Lower Clapton Road, Hackney E5 8EQ
thewindsorcastleclapton.com • +44 2089856096
Open 7 days • ££££

30 The Adam & Eve

Recommended by Rosie Birkett, Chloe Sachdev

"Serves meals made with farm-sourced produce from Cornwall"—*RB*

"The quality of the standout Sunday roast is, in part, thanks to the kitchen's collaboration with The Cornwall Project, a partnership between Cornish suppliers and some of London's best kitchens"—*CS*

155 Homerton High Street, Hackney E9 6AS
adamandevepub.com • +44 2089851494
Open 7 days • ££££

③ The Bull & Gate

Recommended by Catherine & Gavin Hanly

"The best Sunday roast we've had in London. Huge Yorkshire puddings, wonderful roast beef and lashings of intensely flavoured gravy. Best of all you get to walk off your excesses on Hampstead Heath afterwards"
—C&GH

389 Kentish Town Road,
Kentish Town NW5 2TJ
bullandgatenw5.co.uk
+44 2034370905
Open 7 days • ££££

㉜ The Bull & Last

Recommended by Joanne Gould

"Cosy, unpretentious, incredible and imaginative food. The Sunday roasts are particularly good"—*JG*

Ideally situated for Londoners who are just about to walk over Hampstead Heath and require fortification, this popular gastropub serves restaurant-quality British food in some style. The Sunday lunch is renowned – booking in advance is essential, though there's often room at the bar for a pint and an exceptional Scotch egg.

168 Highgate Road, Highgate NW5 1QS
thebullandlast.co.uk • +44 2072673641
Open 7 days • ££££

SMALL PLATES

Over the last ten years, the small plates way of eating has become a massive trend in London. So much so, it can be seemingly impossible to find a new restaurant with a menu based on the classic starter, main, dessert structure. Rather than each individual diner being restricted to choosing three dishes to make up a meal, the table is encouraged to jointly order a scattering of dishes to share. Usually that'll mean selecting four or five dishes per person; some micro-bites, some more significant. These are served as and when they're ready, and are eaten communally by the table.

This style of dining isn't for everyone. But casting cynicism aside, it is deservedly popular. It's informal, convivial and accessible, and because as twos, threes and fours we can all pick at a wide variety of dishes, flavours and ingredients, there's less chance of food envy.

London's myriad small plates offerings cover a variety of different cuisines – from British, through Middle Eastern, Taiwanese, French, Italian and, of course, the original Spanish tapas. They tend to be in busy central areas, and don't tend to take bookings as the format requires a constant flow of bums on seats; you may need to queue, but a corollary of this is that the best of them are always vibrant and lively.

Many of the city's most innovative and successful restaurants of recent years have followed the small plates route, and Londoners find them to be a brilliant place to meet after work or on a date – where a drink and a snack can somehow progress to a full and very enjoyable meal.

See also Bao (page 67), Dishoom (page 56), Kricket (page 54), Madame D (page 59)

33 The Palomar

Recommended by Joanne Gould

"I like the fact that you can sit at the bar and chat to the chefs, and the food is all super modern and well thought out. The octopus is a highlight (when it's on the menu). You must get the bread too. Fab cocktails to accompany and cool music" —*JG*

34 Rupert Street, Covent Garden W1D 6DN
thepalomar.co.uk • +44 2074398777
Open 7 days • ££££

34 Bocca di Lupo

Recommended by Sharlene Carpenter, George Reynolds

"Bocca di Lupo is one of the best Italian restaurants in London, but its real genius lies in the ability to order many of its dishes in both small and large format. Pastas are excellent (especially the tortellini); there are some fine lighter options like the now legendary shaved radish with pecorino and truffle oil. But (as the Romans knew so well) the best stuff comes either out of the fryer or from quarters of the animal that other, wimpier eaters might pass over entirely – both combine in my desert island dish, lamb's sweetbreads fried with lemon and artichoke"—*GR*

12 Archer Street, Soho W1D 7BB
boccadilupo.com • +44 2077342223
Open 7 days • £££££

35 Ceviche

Recommended by Celia Brooks

"There are several branches of this Peruvian bistro around London, but I especially like this one in a restored historic dining room near Old Street roundabout. Each small dish is perfectly formed with high impact flavour and colour. I love their authentic yet modern use of sweet and punchy Aji Amarillo chillies, avocados, beetroot and cassava, plus ceviche of course. These are beautifully executed Peruvian dishes (with some Japanese Nikkei influence) I could probably never recreate at home. The pisco sours are to die for"—*CB*

2 Baldwin Street, Shoreditch EC1V 9NU
(see website for other locations)
cevicheuk.com • +44 2033279463
Open 7 days • £££££

36 Hopscotch

Recommended by Kar-Shing Tong

"Located in trendy Brick Lane, the atmosphere is always relaxed and makes for a pleasant dining experience as you tuck into plates influenced by the Middle East"—*KST*

202 Brick Lane, Shoreditch E1 6SA
hopscotchldn.com • +44 2038767358
Open 7 days • ££££

㊲ Barrafina

Recommended by Catherine & Gavin Hanly, Ed Smith

"Sit at the bar at one of the Barrafinas and it's almost as though you've been teleported to Barcelona. The kitchen staff and waiters call to each other in Spanish, creating a hustle and buzz that would guarantee a good meal, even if the food wasn't remarkable; though as it happens that side of things generally is. There are superlative Spanish omelettes and the daily specials are always worth looking out for. But some of the slow-cooked meat and chargrilled offal options are often the most finger-licking of the small plates"—*ES*

26–27 Dean Street, Soho W1D 3LL
(see website for other locations)
barrafina.co.uk • +44 2074379585
Open 7 days • ££££

③⑧ Kiln

Recommended by Catherine & Gavin Hanly

"Kiln in Soho is a must-visit" —*C&GH*

At Kiln, Thai flavours and British ingredients are combined with skill and cooked in clay pots and over wood-fired stoves. Diners at the ground floor, no-bookings bar can watch the action of the open kitchen, while groups of four or more can make reservations in the dining room downstairs. Casual, stylish and tongue-numbing.

58 Brewer Street, Soho W1F 9TL
kilnsoho.com
Open 7 days • ££££

39 Naughty Piglets

Recommended by Victoria Stewart

"The menu changes relatively often and it's usually so interesting you want to order the whole lot and share it between you"—*VS*

Creative, small plates in an atmospheric Brixton bistro. The food embraces international influences, crossing classic French and British techniques and ingredients with those from much further east – confit duck served with plums and daikon, pork belly and Korean spices. It's eclectic but also excellent. One for fans of natural wines too.

28 Brixton Water Lane, Brixton SW2 1PE
(see website for other locations)
naughtypiglets.co.uk • +44 2072747796
Closed Sunday • ££££

40 Casita Andina

Recommended by Victoria Stewart

"You can take almost anyone to this Peruvian restaurant – I've eaten there with my mum, business colleagues, friends and a date – and it's really good fun. The pisco sours and the ceviche are some of the best in the city, and the servers are unendingly friendly, which really makes you leave on a high"—*VS*

31 Great Windmill Street, Soho W1D 7LP
andinalondon.com • +44 2033279464
Open 7 days • ££££

CURRY

Going for a curry is a particularly British thing to do. Historically (well, since the 1970s), that meant visiting the local Bangladeshi restaurant for a *pasanda*, *korma*, *madras*, *tikka masala* or *jalfrezi*, all made from the same base sauce, but tweaked at the last minute to suit the customer. Add poppadoms, some naan bread, maybe a *saag aloo* and definitely lager, and that's a classic night out.

In London there are still a vast number of family-run neighbourhood Indian restaurants. Whitechapel hosts a cluster of excellent canteen-style restaurants, and Brick Lane in East London has long been famed as a curry destination. But times are changing and you would do well to ignore convention (and that particular street) and look instead to some of the more recently opened restaurants, which take a more contemporary approach towards, and perhaps serve a more authentic version of, the varied food from across India, Bangladesh, Sri Lanka and Pakistan.

The top-end restaurants tend to be in areas like Mayfair and Marylebone – prices suit the postcodes, but then an evening at places like Jamavar (page 59) and Gymkhana (page 58) will be as fine and gilded as in any restaurant in London.

Elsewhere, in more informal, central and east areas of the city such as Soho, Covent Garden and Spitalfields, you can find thoroughly modern, stylish, mid-priced Indian restaurants. Some of these are successful chains focusing on timeless Indian dishes and tradition, like the impressively atmospheric Dishoom (page 56). Others present their own fresh and unique take on Indian spicing, or a specific style of dish, often resulting in some of the most extraordinarily flavoursome mouthfuls of food anywhere in London.

41 DUM Biryani House

Recommended by George Reynolds

"Other people will recommend Gymkhana (page 58), which is indeed fabulous. But for the same level of skill – and the same intense flavours – for about a quarter of the price, Dhruv Mittal's basement biryani shack in a weird part of Soho is a true hidden gem. Mittal has an impressive fine dining pedigree and you can taste the attention to detail, particularly in the small plates (all excellent, and really quite spicy) that precede the main event. Perversely, I haven't always found joy with the signature dish, but it's undeniably generous – and, at these prices, an absolute steal"—*GR*

187B Wardour Street, Soho W1F 8ZB
dumlondon.com • +44 2036380974
Open 7 days • £££

42 Gunpowder

Recommended by Catherine & Gavin Hanly, Kar-Shing Tong

"Places like Gunpowder show us that there's so much potential still to be unlocked in Indian cooking in this city"—*C&GH*

"Gunpowder for me is taking Indian food in London to another level. Located a stone's throw away from Brick Lane, the food is worlds apart from what is typically on offer at London's most famous haunt for Indian food"—*KST*

11 White's Row, Spitalfields E1 7NF
gunpowderlondon.com • +44 2074260542
Closed Sunday • £££

43 Kricket

Recommended by Liz & Max Haarala Hamilton, Catherine & Gavin Hanly, Chloe Sachdev

"A British twist on classic Indian with standout dishes such as Keralan fried chicken with curry leaf mayonnaise"—CS

12 Denman Street, Soho W1D 7HH
kricket.co.uk
Open 7 days • ££££

44 Dishoom

Recommended by Rosie Birkett, Sharlene Carpenter, Chloe Sachdev

"I adore Dishoom. It's a small group of Indian restaurants modelled on Mumbai's extraordinary Parsi cafés, and the food is fantastic and incredibly well priced. Expect bowls of the creamiest black dahl and house specials like *bhel puri* – a colourful, textural mix of puffed rice with tamarind, crispy vermicelli, chillies and pomegranates"—*RB*

"Dishoom is my go-to for Indian comfort food. If I'm not there in the morning for breakfast (for bottomless chai and bacon and egg naans) the chicken ruby curry is a firm favourite for dinner"—*CS*

7 Boundary Street, Shoreditch E2 7JE
(see website for other locations)
dishoom.com • +44 2074209324
Open 7 days • ££££

45 Gymkhana

Recommended by Catherine & Gavin Hanly, Ed Smith

"When Gymkhana opened it set a new bar for medium to high-end Indian restaurants. The room is plush and service first rate, and whereas 'posh' curry used to be smudges and slate plates, this is just an array of perfectly spiced fish, meat and game served without too much fuss from the tandoor or in curry form. The cocktails are excellent too. At the top end of pricing (though there are lunch and early evening set menus), but worth it"—ES

42 Albemarle Street, Mayfair W1S 4JH
gymkhanalondon.com • +44 2030115900
Closed Sunday • ££££

46 Jamavar

Recommended by Catherine & Gavin Hanly, Ed Smith

"A favourite for a fine-dining approach"—*C&GH*

The refined, near opulent surroundings of this high-end Indian restaurant match regally spiced dishes and the Mayfair postcode. Their menus are influenced by a range of India's regional cuisines, to great success. The wine list is taken seriously, too.

8 Mount Street, Mayfair W1K 3NF
jamavarrestaurants.com • +44 2074991800
Closed Sunday • ££££

47 Madame D

Recommended by Catherine & Gavin Hanly

"We like Madame D in the City for a more grungy style, which is playing with the classics. It shows how far Indian cuisine has come"—*C&GH*

76 Commercial Street, The City E1 6LY
madame-d.com • +44 2072471341
Closed Sunday and Monday • ££££

NOODLES

There's huge variety in the theme of Noodles, as potentially it covers Japanese *udon* and *ramen*, Chinese hand-pulled noodles, Vietnamese *pho* and *bun*, Malaysian *laksa* and more. But noodle bars are united in that they reflect London's acceptance of and appetite for a truly global kitchen. They also all sit within the much-improved "fast casual" end of the city's restaurant market that allows locals to dine out well with friends (or solo) for less than £20 a head.

You don't need to walk too far around central Soho, Holborn and Piccadilly to find a tangle of decent noodles swimming in an umami-rich broth. Further, most of the shiny "glass box" developments at the base of office blocks in central and east London contain solid noodle brands too. Most offer pre-noodle bites, like spiced or fish sauce-laced chicken wings, marinated but still raw sashimi, or pot-sticker dumplings. Whether you indulge in those or not, your bowl of buckwheat *soba*, rice vermicelli or *ramen* will arrive relatively quickly; so it's ideal for a brief lunch pit stop, or as a book-end to an evening. These are slick, functional restaurants. Never unwelcoming, but also not typically decked out for the long haul – a reflection of the fact that the food on offer isn't necessarily of a type that you or your fellow customers will languish over for hours.

Having said that you should be able to stumble across the increasing number of decent central options, though the real gems do need to be aimed at, otherwise you'll miss out on the deepest, most layered *tonkotsu ramen*, the feistiest hand-pulled noodles, or the bounciest, yet totally serene *udon*.

Pound for pound, London's noodles offer some of the most rewarding eating in town. Slurp on.

See also Silk Road (page 67)

48 Kanada-Ya

Recommended by Ed Smith

"A bundle of decent *ramen* restaurants have sprung up over the last five years or so. Kanada-Ya, an import from Yukuhashi, Japan, is my favourite of the current crop, and their queues suggest I'm not alone. The pork and chicken broth is consistently excellent (smooth with layers of flavour) and I love, in particular, the chilli Gekikara option. Always restorative and satisfying"—*ES*

64 St Giles High Street, Covent Garden WC2H 8LE
(see website for other locations)
kanada-ya.com • +44 2072400232
Open 7 days • £££

49 Koya Bar

Recommended by Ed Smith

"To my mind the best place for noodles in London AND one of the best places to eat full stop. The *udon* are firm and bouncy; the broths and sauces refined and serene; and the specials board, which always features ingenious Japanese takes on British seasonal ingredients, a constant treat, whether breakfast, lunch or dinner. Great that there's now a Koya in the City, as well as this Soho gem"—ES

50 Frith Street, Soho W1D 4SQ
(see website for other locations)
koyabar.co.uk
Open 7 days • £££

50 Salvation in Noodles

Recommended by Kar-Shing Tong

"My go-to place for noodles in London. It never fails to satisfy on both the food and general vibes" —*KST*

No-frills decor, but buckets of flavour at this modern Vietnamese noodle shack, which offers a range of enjoyable noodle soups – both flat rice noodle (*pho*) and vermicelli (*bun*) fans are catered for – as well as cold noodle salads topped with the likes of spiced pork patties (*bun nem nuong*) and beef in betel leaves (*bun bo la lot*). They've a crowd-pleasing set of pre-noodle snacks for sharing too.

122 Balls Pond, Dalston N1 4AE
(see website for other locations)
salvationinnoodles.co.uk • +44 2072544534
Open 7 days • £££££

51 Baozi Inn

Recommended by Liz & Max Haarala Hamilton

"Go for the Dan Dan noodles" —*L&MHH*

A small and always busy restaurant on the bustling Newport Court stretch of Chinatown, which specialises in Sichuanese street food. Expect good value skewered meats and dense pork buns (both available to go from an outdoor counter too), as well as Dan Dan noodles – cold noodles with sesame chicken and plenty of heat from tongue-tingling Sichuan peppercorns.

26 Newport Court, Chinatown WC2H 7JS
baoziinn.com • +44 2072876877
Open 7 days • £££££

52 Mien Tay

Recommended by Chloe Sachdev

"I always love a bowl of *pho*. There's no shortage of great authentic Vietnamese on Kingsland Road but my go-to is Mien Tay"—*CS*

122 Kingsland Road, Shoreditch E2 8DP
(see website for other locations)
mientay.co.uk • +44 2077293074
Open 7 days • ££££

CHINESE

The area between Leicester Square and Soho known as Chinatown is a high-spirited, coruscating zone – its borders indicated by large red and gold ornamental arches. Visitors bustle between restaurants and shops at all times of day and night, many transfixed by the glazed ducks and dumpling makers providing theatre from behind glazed windows. The supermarkets and quick, casual bites (steamed buns, dumplings, fried chicken and sweet treats) are worth the journey and crowds. If you're after a restaurant experience, though, you might do better to head elsewhere.

The options for eating Chinese food in London have moved on from generic Cantonese (or British versions of it), to the sweet, sour, spicy and fiery nuances that specific regional cooking provides. Well represented sub-categories of Chinese cuisine include Taiwanese, Sichuanese and Hunanese; your taste buds will be transported and rewarded in these restaurants if you stick to the marked house specials, or ask what is unique to their locality.

If you're after dumplings then the city provides a number of options. A clutch of mid-level Cantonese restaurants serve dim sum at lunchtime. Their massive rooms (a number of which are in the Baker Street area) house large tables with spinning middles, to which baskets of steamed and fried dumplings, buns, glutinous rolls and pastries are brought in quick order, lubricated by endless cups of fragrant tea. High-end Chinese restaurants in central and west London sites offer a very fine, delicate-skinned version of the same. Elsewhere, in lower-key areas and at street food markets (page 78), there are an increasing number of home-style dumpling bars and counters, offering rustic but ultimately very pleasing steamed parcels for a fraction of the price.

See also Baozi Inn (page 64), Royal China Club (page 18), Yauatcha (page 125)

53 Bao

Recommended by Ed Smith

"Pillow-soft Taiwanese steamed buns are a significant draw (confit pork is my preference). But I love Bao Fitzrovia for their ingenious and mouth-watering drinking snacks, grills and stews. Every bite is a sensory explosion, from the chicken chop with soy-cured egg through to Mapo aubergine. They use quality British ingredients and add Chinese flavourings to awesome effect"—*ES*

31 Windmill Street, Fitzrovia W1T 2JN
(see website for other locations)
baolondon.com • +44 2030111632
Closed Sunday • ££££

54 Hunan

Recommended by George Reynolds

"Hunan is in Belgravia, which is another way of saying it's not cheap. But surrender to the cost and the concept – there is no menu; flag dietary restrictions upfront – and you will be sumptuously rewarded for your courage with a tasting menu comprising dozens of gorgeous small bites rooted in the Hunan region but content, too, to range wider across China. One for making special occasions even more so"—*GR*

51 Pimlico Road, Belgravia SW1W 8NE
hunanlondon.com • +44 2077305712
Closed Sunday • ££££

55 Silk Road

Recommended by Kar-Shing Tong

"Silk Road has long been a personal favourite of mine. Food here is super affordable but also very delicious"—*KST*

A Camberwell institution, Silk Road's noodles and stews are rooted in the Xinjiang cuisine of north-western China. The setting is basic, the food anything but: hand-pulled noodles, sweet home-style aubergine, cumin dusted lamb skewers, huge plates of spiced chicken and aromatic shredded pork. It always hits the spot and is exceptional value. Queues are likely, but service is quick.

49 Camberwell Church Street, Camberwell SE5 8TR
+44 2077034832
Open 7 days • ££££

56 Mamalan

Recommended by Liz & Max Haarala Hamilton

"For amazing dumplings and really authentic Beijing street food" *—L&MHH*

Unit 9, Avant Garde, Shoreditch E1 6GU
(see website for other locations)
mamalan.co.uk • +44 2077399559
Open 7 days • ££££

57 XU

Recommended by Chloe Sachdev

"For inventive upmarket Taiwanese fare in a Wes Anderson-like setting, try XU (pronounced *shu*) from the folks behind the ever-popular Bao (page 67)" —*CS*

30 Rupert Street, Soho W1D 6DL
xulondon.com • +44 2033198147
Closed Sunday • ££££

58 Chilli Cool

Recommended by Ed Smith

"For a no-frills, but plenty of heat experience, try Chilli Cool near King's Cross. The café-style restaurant presents classic Sichuanese tongue-numbing dishes (like dry-fried beans and minced pork; sweet, sour, spicy black fungus; rip-snorting beef in chilli oil; and sweat-inducing Kung Pao chicken) reliably well and without fuss. It feels authentic and is keenly priced"—*ES*

15 Leigh Street, King's Cross WC1H 9EW
chillicool.co.uk • +44 207383 3135
Open 7 days • £££ £

59 Shikumen

Recommended by Ed Smith

"Shikumen now have restaurants in Ealing, Shepherd's Bush, Aldgate and Finchley Road. Which means west, north and east London have access to reliable, reasonably priced mid-range dim sum. But I like Shikumen because (unusually for London), there doesn't appear to be a weak link across the menu, whether steamed dumpling, *char siew bun*, turnip cake or baked puff"—*ES*

58 Shepherd's Bush Green, Shepherd's Bush W12 8QE
(see website for other locations)
shikumen.co.uk • +44 2087499978
Open 7 days • ££ ££

60 Leong's Legend

Recommended by Chloe Sachdev

"If you don't mind indifferent and speedy service, Leong's Legends in Chinatown has excellent soupy dumplings and hotpot"—*CS*

39 Gerrard Street, Chinatown W1D 5QD
Open 7 days • £££ £

MANGAL

There are around 500,000 people of Turkish and Turkish Cypriot origin in London. Most live in north and north-east boroughs, in areas such as Dalston, Stoke Newington and Harringay, though strong communities are evident in south-east London too. It's to zone two, three and beyond, then, that you should head when you feel the urge for a grilled meat and charred vegetable feast – for the Turks are masters of cooking over white-hot coals.

Enter a busy mangal or *ocakbasi* (fireside) restaurant, and you'll see generous skewers of marinated chicken and lamb, long, minced *adana* kebabs, lamb chops, chicken wings, quail and offal, all under a billowing cloud of smoke that's whisked away by one of the city's best extraction units. Greens are not front and centre, but sides like charred peppers and tomatoes, and burnt onions drenched with mouth-puckering pomegranate molasses are on offer, and help to cut through the richness of all the protein. Portions are generous and most restaurants send complimentary meze and salads while your meat is being grilled.

Many modern restaurants in central London celebrate the fact they cook over fire. It could be argued that Turkish mangal restaurants got there first, and may still do it best. There's a place for both, of course, with the traditional Turkish option guaranteeing a great value evening meal of mammoth proportions.

61 Black Axe Mangal

Recommended by Catherine & Gavin Hanly, George Reynolds, Ed Smith

"Don't take your elderly relatives: the music is loud (LOUD) heavy metal, and there are drawings of male and female genitalia on the floor. But the food – particularly the flatbreads, and the rave-culture riffs on kebab-house classics – is worth any amount of discomfort; former St John (page 27) head chef Lee Tiernan knows exactly what he's doing. Like Metallica, it has an irresistible power and intensity; like sex, it's pure, eye-rolling pleasure. Like sex with me, it's often over far, far too soon"—*GR*

156 Canonbury Road, Islington N1 2UP
blackaxemangal.com
Open 7 days • ££££

⓺ Testi

Recommended by Rosie Birkett, Chloe Sachdev

"Testi in Stoke Newington is the one. It has a smoking mangal grill and is always buzzing with diners who come for the juicy chicken shish, charred onion and turnip juice salad and grilled bread which is dredged with the grilled meat juices. This place never disappoints and is very reasonably priced"—*RB*

"A fantastic Turkish neighbourhood *ocakbasi* in Stoke Newington that is great value for money. The marinated grilled lamb chops and *sucuk* (Turkish sausage) are winners. Although, I'm yet to brave the house speciality of pan-fried lamb's testicles..."—*CS*

36 Stoke Newington High Street, Stoke Newington N16 7PL
testirestaurant.co.uk • +44 2072493979
Open 7 days • ££££

63 Antepliler

Recommended by Celia Brooks

"Take a trip down to Green Lanes any time of day or night for amazing Turkish food. Follow the aroma of barbecue smoke wafting from the multiple *ocakbasi* restaurants and you can hardly go wrong. In my opinion, one of the best restaurants in that area is Antepliler. You can get enormous platters of barbecued meat which come with warm flatbread, dips, and heaps of fresh herby salad, but I always go for a selection of the delectable meze such as fresh crisp falafel, grilled aubergines and peppers in yoghurt"—*CB*

46 Grand Parade, Green Lanes, Harringay N4 1AG
+44 2088025588
Open 7 days • £££E

64 Gökyüzü

Recommended by Celia Brooks, Ed Smith

"Green Lanes in Harringay is not short of authentic Turkish restaurants, however Gökyüzü is the place to head for generous platters of chargrilled kebabs, chops, wings and ribs and freshly baked Turkish breads; each item just that level beyond their competition. A must if you're in the area and keen on a smoky feast, and still worth a journey if not"—*ES*

26–28 Grand Parade, Green Lanes, Harringay N4 1LG
(see website for other locations)
gokyuzurestaurant.co.uk • +44 2082118406
Open 7 days • £££E

65 Likya

Recommended by Joanne Gould

"The best kebab I've ever had. The doner is seasoned amazingly and the *ocakbasi* grill delivers the right flame-grill flavour if you're going for a shish skewer. Great for eating in or taking away and very reasonably priced. I can hardly walk past this place without going in"—*JG*

68–70 Golders Green Road, Golders Green NW11 8LN
likya.co.uk • +44 2084557171
Open 7 days • ££££

STREET FOOD

Historically it's all inclement weather, dodgy hotdogs and burgers of indeterminable origin. Yet London can now be added to the list of the world's great street food cities.

The scene took off around a decade ago – an affordable and innovative response, perhaps, to a cocktail of financial crisis, rising restaurant rents and the burgeoning influence of social media. Traders found that they could start ambitious and innovative food businesses without possessing the traditional cash and experience, and that there was a young and appreciative audience gagging for informal grub on the go. Subsequently, purchasing hot food from the back of converted vans or off wobbly tables moved from being a convenience to a hotly anticipated activity. The scene is a fluid one, with its star players regularly changing, so this guide aims to recommend destinations and curators, rather than individual stalls.

London's street food can be found in well-curated public spaces close to office worker- and student-heavy areas. There are hawker centre and food hall-style spaces as well, some open for lunch, many just in the evening towards the end of the week and at weekends – here the atmosphere and drinks are as big a feature as the food. Keep your eyes on kerbfood.com and streetfeast.com for some of the latest destinations.

And there are pleasingly ramshackle options too, where actual, real-life, unadulterated street markets host a jumble of trendy and traditional foods, in amongst traders selling underwear, groceries and handbags.

See also MARKETS (page 110)

66 Maltby Street Market

Recommended by Victoria Stewart

"I do find myself returning repeatedly to Maltby Street Market for whatever's on that day. That's either because I know I can trust what I'm getting – and I can have a chat with the traders – or because there'll always be something new to try"—*VS*

41 Maltby Street, Southwark SE1 3PA
maltby.st
Open Saturday and Sunday • £££f

67 Leather Lane Market

Recommended by George Reynolds

"Street food in other countries is not a commodity that can be packaged up and sold in giant fake Hawker Houses and Street Feasts; it is food that normal people eat, just on the street. Leather Lane is one such street: a local affair, where myriad falafel stands and jerk chicken joints rub shoulders with greengrocers and deeply unlovely fashion labels. Most of the food is great, but not much of it is fancy – and don't even think about trying to Instagram it"—GR

Leather Lane, Clerkenwell EC1N 7TJ
leatherlanestars.com
Open Monday to Friday • £££££

68 Druid Street Market

Recommended by Catherine & Gavin Hanly

"It's our favourite place to hang out and eat street food in London. It can be packed, but if you know where to go, there are side streets with pockets of artisan producers – it's got a great atmosphere and is a good alternative to nearby Borough Market (page 114)"—C&GH

126 Druid Street, Bermondsey SE1 2HH
Open Saturday • £££££

69 Dinerama

Recommended by Chloe Sachdev

"Dinerama has everything you could possibly want, from pizza to burgers and wine bars. There's even a vodka energy bar pumping out vodka Redbull slushies… and a German Sex Dungeon (that's actually a craft can and whisky shot bar)"—CS

19 Great Eastern Street, Shoreditch EC2A 3EJ
streetfeast.com
Opening times variable • £££££

⑦⓪ KERB

Recommended by Catherine & Gavin Hanly, Ed Smith

"KERB in King's Cross hosts an ever-changing roster of traders. There's Granary Square and the canal nearby if you fancy eating in the sun (if you're lucky)"—*C&GH*

"Arguably the instigator of a movement, and certainly an arbiter of quality and incubator of talent. Their destinations are most often in office worker- and student-heavy environs (King's Cross, The Gherkin, London Bridge, Southbank), though they also run weekend-long and evening events"—*ES*

See website for locations
kerbfood.com
Opening times variable • £££

ICE CREAM

Hang around a park or residential neighbourhood long enough over the summer months, and you'll hear the tinny, jangling music of an ice cream van, calling kids (of all ages) like London's very own Pied Piper. These mobile freezers are famous for their cones of Mr Whippy soft serve and 99 Flakes, as well as an assortment of classic iced lollies. It's a British thing. A London thing. But there's better to be had – whether the sun is indeed shining or there's a chill in the air.

This is because there's a growing breed of new wave ice cream vans and trolleys, which are generally to be found at street food hubs (page 78) and farmers' markets (page 110), though some also have their glacial goodies stocked in independent delicatessens and trendy cafés. The likes of Nonna's (opposite) make small batches of ices using the best organic milk and cream, along with inspired combinations of seasonal ingredients, and even flavours from local producers (coffee, stout and so on). It's like the city's craft food scene frozen in time inside a cardboard container, which is an encapsulation that's well worth trying.

Elsewhere, on busy high streets and in central spots like Soho and Covent Garden, there are a clutch of quality gelaterias and ice cream bars. Again, the appearance of seasonal ingredients on their ever changing menus are an indicator that you're in good hands. Happily, you should be able to both browse the open tubs of enticing colours and flavours, and try a few spoonfuls before you buy. The locations and trading hours of these shops tend to mean they're as handy for second breakfast or elevenses as they are the perfect afternoon pit stop, palate cleanser or dessert to follow lunch or dinner. No one will judge you for requesting the maximum number of scoops.

⑦ Gelateria 3Bis

Recommended by Joanne Gould, Kar-Shing Tong

"I went to the original in Rimini, Italy and got a bit obsessed. The gelato is just as good in this branch"—JG

"3Bis in Borough Market is a personal favourite of mine. Flavours here are always interesting and taste delightful"—KST

4 Park Street, Borough Market SE1 9AB
(see website for other locations)
gelateria3bis.co.uk
Open 7 days • £££££

⑦ Nonna's Gelato

Recommended by Ed Smith

"I love Nonna's approach to ice cream: small batch gelato that makes the most of organic Jersey cow milk and cream and seasonal ingredients – a kind of Italian-British fusion. The Kentish cobnut ice cream and London brewers Five Points dark beer and chocolate ripple stand out, though options change all the time. As far as I'm concerned, their roving stalls and carts – found at KERB (page 81) and other markets – are the new ice cream van"—ES

See website for locations
nonnasgelato.com
Opening times variable • £££££

⑦ Chin Chin Labs

Recommended by Sharlene Carpenter, Catherine & Gavin Hanly

"They do liquid nitrogen ice cream in an array of flavours and you get to pick your own toppings – try the burnt butter caramel ice cream sandwiched between two homemade chocolate chip cookies"—SC

"Take the kids (hell, go even if you're not travelling with kids) to the original Chin Chin Labs in Camden for their nitro ice cream experience"—C&GH

49–50 Camden Lock Place, Camden NW1 8AF
(see website for other locations)
chinchinlabs.com
Open 7 days • £££££

74 Gelupo

Recommended by Joanne Gould, George Reynolds, Ed Smith, Victoria Stewart

"Jacob Kenedy popularised proper Italian-style gelato when he opened Gelupo on Archer Street in 2010; while little pots of the stuff have been popping up in right-minded delicatessens across the city, the flagship store is still the best place to get it. The offering changes with the seasons – light, intensely flavoured granita in the summer; deep, dark hot chocolate enriched with hazelnut cream in winter – but a few stalwarts are always worth trying: the pistachio, or the eye-opening espresso *sorbetto*. Lethally, they also do giant containers of the most popular flavours to take home"—*GR*

7 Archer Street, Soho W1D 7AU
gelupo.com • +44 2072875555
Open 7 days • ££££

⑦⑤ Four Winters

Recommended by Celia Brooks

"I'm a big fan of this relatively new ice cream and frozen yoghurt shop where they freeze it to order using a very theatrical infusion of liquid nitrogen and a Kitchen Aid! The instant freezing means that crystals don't form, so it's the creamiest ice cream imaginable. Plus they use all-natural ingredients and no added sugar, and there are some wonderfully wacky flavours like honey and chilli"—*CB*

53 Brewer Street, Soho W1F 9UY
(see website for other locations)
fourwinters.co • +44 2077346667
Open 7 days • £££f

COCKTAILS

London's cocktail scene is far from homogeneous. Indeed it's true to say that there are a number of different styles of bar, each of which suits a different drinking mood.

One is the classic, luxury hotel bar in Mayfair or the West End. The setting for your martini, whisky sour or daiquiri is sheer luxe: marble surfaces, silver shakers, impeccably dressed bar staff, the furnishings of your dreams and maybe a live pianist setting the mood. Here classic cocktails are mixed with precision and served with class, style and deference. It's a touch of decadence at the start or end of an evening.

Another is the innovative, hipster option. Acclaimed tastemakers lend their expertise, palates and wizardry to refined cocktails – tinctures, herbal infusions and essences distilled using centrifugal force are blended into spirits with scientific precision and served sub zero. Venues tend to be small, discreet and edgy. There are a handful in central London basements, though increasingly these bars are in younger neighbourhoods like Shoreditch and Dalston. Signage will be subtle – they're for those in the know and some require you to book ahead.

A third option is to be found within fashionable restaurants, where the drinks menu rivals the food's for creativity. Expect a twist on a negroni, house-blended vermouth, and gin-based aperitifs using a derivative of chef's mise en place. You don't need to be a diner – often there's an area separate to the main dining room, with its own abridged menu of snacks and small plates, and alternative clientele. Restaurants with these sorts of bars attached tend to be found in Shoreditch and Mayfair, again, as well as Soho, Covent Garden and Clerkenwell.

⑦⑥ Sager + Wilde

Recommended by Chloe Sachdev

"Bethnal Green has become something of cocktail hub for clued-in industry folk. Sager + Wilde does an especially good olive oil old fashioned. Or go for wine with toasties (it's a thing)"—*CS*

Arch 250 Paradise Row, Bethnal Green E2 9LE
(see website for other locations)
sagerandwilde.com • +44 2076130478
Open 7 days • ££££

77 Dukes Bar

Recommended by Ed Smith

"There is no better start to an evening, nor is there a better (or more potent) martini, than that shaken by Alessandro Palazzi at Dukes Bar. The bar is intimate, personal, classy and timeless, and the drinks match that setting. This is London hospitality of a bygone era; very cool, without seemingly trying to be, and totally intoxicating"—*ES*

35 St James's Place, St James's SW1A 1NY
dukeshotel.com • +44 2074914840
Open 7 days • ££££

78 Luca Bar

Recommended by Ed Smith

"The British-Italian restaurant from the people behind The Clove Club (page 30) has a beautiful bar at the front of the building. This features a different food menu to that served in the main (and equally chic) dining room, as well as a classy cocktail list. I'm partial to their gin- and/or Campari-based concoctions. It's an elegant place to sit, sip and eat. Worth booking ahead, though you could chance an early evening sharpener or a nightcap later on"—*ES*

88 St John Street, Clerkenwell EC1M 4EH
luca.restaurant
Closed Sunday • ££££

79 Claridge's

Recommended by Catherine & Gavin Hanly

"We do love a hotel cocktail bar and probably the one we've been going to the longest is the bar at Claridge's. We were lucky enough to stay overnight here not that long ago and the martini they made for us in the wee small hours was a knockout – literally"—*C&GH*

Brook Street, Mayfair W1K 4HR
claridges.co.uk • +44 2076298860
Open 7 days • ££££

⑧⓪ Nightjar

Recommended by Victoria Stewart

"I've had many good nights – and cocktails – at Nightjar" —*VS*

A speakeasy-style cocktail bar on the edge of Shoreditch, with inventive drinks and live jazz and swing after 9pm. They offer table service only and it's best to book to reserve seats, but the ambience and sense of occasion make advance planning worth it.

129 City Road, Shoreditch EC1V 1JB
barnightjar.com • +44 2072534101
Open 7 days • ££££

81 Every Cloud

Recommended by George Reynolds

"Come for the hilariously written menu, stay for what are consistently the best, most creative cocktails in London. Stay even longer, because not only do these guys know their stuff, they're entirely without pretension or affect (You want a beer? Have a beer!) and are gracious, generous, funny hosts. And spend a night curled up in a ball on the floor, because after your first Martiny – it's a frozen martini from a Heath Robinsoned Jagermeister dispenser, only very small! – you'll have another, and another, and maybe one more. Good night"—*GR*

11 Morning Lane, Hackney E9 6NU
everycloudbar.com • +44 2034419850
Open 7 days • £££££

WINE BARS

There are numerous generic, hard-surfaced rooms in the City's financial and theatreland districts which act as fly-traps for besuited workers at Happy Hour, or other unsuspecting punters looking for something that isn't quite a pub. Large windows onto the street, blackboards denoting five or six varietals sold in small, medium or large glasses – these could certainly be classified as bars, and they definitely sell wine. But in recent years a new type of establishment has appeared, which aims to please serious oenophiles and a new, more discerning breed of wine drinker.

A number of these bars are found in unsuspecting areas out in zones two, three and four, under railway arches and on streets that are not yet up-and-coming. These, more often than not, focus on natural wine – made by small-scale producers with as little intervention as possible. The crowd tends to be young; often restaurant and wine industry types, all keen on drinking bottles of unadulterated character. Decor tends to be low-key, though you'll still be drinking from the finest glassware, and often have the option of top quality cheese, charcuterie and small plates too.

Other wine-focused venues in more central or established residential zones remain on the side of the chateaus and estates of the old world and traditional methods. Their lists are long and weighty, with a key feature being the use of Coravin bottle openers or dispensers, which allow for a single glass to be poured from a bottle without the rest of it spoiling. So extraordinarily priced rare, vintage and high-end wines become just a little bit more affordable and accessible. It's not only horizontal and vertical tastings and premium grapes – there's usually something for everyone.

82 The Remedy

Recommended by Victoria Stewart

"I like this bar because you can always try something new, and the staff will give you as much or as little explanation as you like. It's also very easy to end up staying longer to work your way through the menu of bar snacks or a platter of British cheese"—VS

124 Cleveland Street, Fitzrovia W1T 6PG
theremedylondon.com • +44 2034893800
Closed Sunday • ££££

83 40 Maltby Street

Recommended by Ed Smith

"The charmingly musty and characterful railway arch setting of this bar-cum-restaurant is entirely apt for the wine served on site. The public front of a natural wine import business is an excellent place to head if you're after the barnyard funk and cloudy wines with personality. It's an organic, unpretentious and convivial place to take on a bottle or two. Happily the food served from their small kitchen is also brilliant"—ES

40 Maltby Street, Southwark SE1 3PA
40maltbystreet.com • +44 2072379247
Open Wednesday to Sunday • ££££

84 Gordon's Wine Bar

Recommended by Joanne Gould

"For cosy red wine and cheese winter nights where you feel you're in some kind of gothic drama; and equally for spilling out onto the street in summer. Always fun. Always packed"—JG

47 Villiers Street, St James's WC2N 6NE
gordonswinebar.com • +44 2079301408
Open 7 days • ££££

85 P. Franco

Recommended by Rosie Birkett, George Reynolds, Chloe Sachdev

"I originally came to P. Franco with no idea that it was a wine bar, seduced via a series of Instagrams of then-chef William Gleave's gorgeous Italianate food. But while Gleave (and a murderers' row of other talented cooks) has now passed through the tiny kitchen at the back of the shop, the wines have remained – natural ones, interesting ones, occasionally challenging ones, all served with endearing Antipodean charm by Phil Bracey and his team"—*GR*

107 Lower Clapton Road, Hackney E5 ONP
pfranco.co.uk • +44 2085334660
Closed Monday • ££££

86 Noble Rot

Recommended by George Reynolds, Chloe Sachdev, Ed Smith

"Housed in a 400-year-old building, it has bags of character, as does the food. Order some oysters to get you in the mood – then game is a particular highlight, as is anything involving smoked eel or slipsole. The wine list is (of course) outstanding" —GR

"The wine list at Noble Rot will satisfy even the hardest to please aficionados. It showcases a cellar of both brilliant unknowns and drops from the world's leading winemakers, meaning there's great value by the glass, as well as jaw-dropping Grand Cru by the bottle. I'm fond of their fondness of brilliant Burgundian Chardonnay and Pinot Noir, plus the lengthy Riesling page. They do everything right, here (including the food). Well worth a visit" —ES

51 Lamb's Conduit Street, Bloomsbury WC1N 3NB
noblerot.co.uk • +44 2072428963
Closed Sunday • ££££

PUBS

Pubs are a crucial part of London's fabric. Indeed they're intertwined with the history and narrative of the city: with numerous watering holes having survived or been rebuilt without haste after the Great Fire of London in 1666; and even more of them apparently once the regular haunt of Charles Dickens.

Every neighbourhood has at least one, if not four, local boozers, often tucked away in unsuspecting backstreets and down cobbled alleyways. And they remain strategic stopping points near the entrances to the Royal Parks, at bends in the river Thames and close to most tube station exits. Basically, it's essential that there's always somewhere convenient in which to buy a pint.

Not all pubs are made equal, though, and it's difficult to put a finger on the winning formula. At some, it's the historic setting that lends an intangible but definite atmosphere. Maybe the discreet corners, log fires and wooden panelling help. Others host a broad selection of dependable ales and modern craft beers, and attract the discerning drinkers. And then there are some that simply have enviable locations – a sun terrace or street onto which punters happily spill out on uncharacteristically balmy evenings. Regardless, you can pretty much tell immediately whether you've picked a good one: the welcome from both bartender and regular is warming, even if unspoken (it's a London thing); the first sip is crisp and refreshing; and you'll not want to leave before having just one more for the road.

See also PUB KITCHEN (page 34), SUNDAY ROAST (page 38)

87 The Southampton Arms

Recommended by Ed Smith

"I like nothing more on an autumn or winter weekend in London than a brisk yomp over Hampstead Heath, followed by a pint or two at the Southampton Arms – an ale and cider house that sells only beers and ciders from small independent breweries (plus a few Scotch eggs and sausage rolls). There's a long bar with multiple taps, a fire, a piano and not much else. If you could bottle the experience you'd make a fortune"—ES

139 Highgate Road, Highgate NW5 1LE
thesouthamptonarms.co.uk
Open 7 days • ££££

88 The Barrowboy & Banker

Recommended by Sharlene Carpenter

"A lovely centrally located Fullers pub near London Bridge. Formerly a bank with a spiral staircase, high ceilings and original features still in place. Try some of their popular ales, including London Pride and ESB. The great thing about this pub is you can sample their ale selection before buying, so you can choose one that is suited to your taste"—SC

6–8 Borough High Street, Borough SE1 9QQ
barrowboy-and-banker.co.uk • +44 2074035415
Open 7 days • ££££

89 The Lamb

Recommended by Ed Smith

"At one end of the picturesque Lamb's Conduit Street is a historic favourite watering hole of Dickens, which has been tastefully renovated with its characterful bar still pride of place. It's an excellent central London pub option, in that it's well located and has one eye on tradition, and the other on a good range of contemporary beer and wine"—ES

94 Lamb's Conduit Street, Bloomsbury WC1N 3LZ
thelamblondon.com • +44 2074050713
Open 7 days • £££

⑨⓪ Chesham Arms

Recommended by Rosie Birkett

"It's a hidden spot off the main drag and has a wonderful atmosphere, with board games, two wood burners and really good local ales and craft beers. You can bring dogs, there's a huge garden out the back and, while they don't do food, you're welcome to order in. It's the best pub in London in my book"—*RB*

15 Mehetabel Road, Hackney E9 6DU
cheshamarms.com • +44 2089866717
Open 7 days • ££££

COFFEE

A sprinkling of early roasters and cafés aside (notably Monmouth, page 106), London's third wave of independent, artisan coffee kicked off around 2005, grew steadily for a couple of years and exploded from 2009 onwards. The influence of Australasian baristas was (and is) strong, and there's still a greater concentration of good coffee to be had in Old Street, Shoreditch and east of those two places than anywhere else. But it's fair to say that you can't move in London now for flat whites, cortados and latte art, not to mention Chemex, V60 or Aeropress drip filters. Which is to say that in 2010 it would have been relatively easy to provide a short list of the best places to get coffee in London without missing any key players; but now the list is so long, many will be miffed not to make the cut.

This doesn't mean a good brew is guaranteed. So it's helpful to know the telltale indicators that suggest you're in line for a decent coffee: the café roasts its own beans, or at least displays bags of stylishly branded coffee on the shelves behind their sleek espresso machine; its tattooed baristas are inherently hip and louche; the interior is trendy and pared-back; and seventy per cent of the seats are taken by laptop-wielding freelancers.

A handful of players have made things easier by opening multiple sites, while retaining a high quality product. There remain excellent soloists, too: one of the originals, Prufrock (page 107), is an essential visit for the coffee geeks.

⑨¹ Allpress

Recommended by Chloe Sachdev

"One of the best roasters in London. I particularly like their Dalston branch for a leisurely weekend brunch as you can always find a table and there's outdoor seating. The eggs and toast aren't bad either. Otherwise I drop by their Redchurch branch in east London for takeaway"—CS

55 Dalston Lane, Dalston E8 2NG
(see website for other locations)
uk.allpressespresso.com • +44 2077491780
Open 7 days • £££££

92 Monmouth

Recommended by Sharlene Carpenter, Joanne Gould

"A strong, full, robust coffee. Staff are knowledgeable about the products they sell. The coffee you buy can be greatly impacted by the milk used – Monmouth knows the importance of this and uses Jersey milk, a higher fat content milk that brings a luxurious sweetness to their coffee"—SC

"Hands down best coffee in London, and the croissants aren't bad either"—JG

2 Park Street, Borough SE1 9AB
(see website for other locations)
monmouthcoffee.co.uk • +44 2072323010
Closed Sunday • £££

93 Grind

Recommended by Kar-Shing Tong

"I always appreciate the Grind locations for the atmosphere as much as the coffee. Always quite edgy with a great soundtrack"—*KST*

213 Old Street, Shoreditch EC1V 9NR
(see website for other locations)
grind.co.uk • +44 2074907490
Open 7 days • £££££

• •

94 Origin

Recommended by Ed Smith

"A handful of quality independent coffee shops and roasters are expanding their number of sites. This is a good thing, but some grow better than others. I'm a fan of Origin, who roast their own beans in the south-west of England" —*ES*

65 Charlotte Road, Shoreditch EC2A 3PE
(see website for other locations)
origincoffee.co.uk
Open 7 days • £££££

• •

95 Prufrock

Recommended by Ed Smith

"Prufrock is one of London's original third-wave coffee shops, and still one of the best. The buzzing, clattering room on Leather Lane takes both espresso and brew bar very seriously, yet the setting is refreshingly neither aloof nor over-styled. In many ways a standard-bearer, I've never had a disappointing coffee there"—*ES*

23–25 Leather Lane, Clerkenwell EC1N 7TE
prufrockcoffee.com • +44 2072420467
Open 7 days • £££££

96 Briki

Recommended by George Reynolds

"Briki is on the corner of Exmouth Market, which means it is in the vicinity of approximately a million other coffee shops, all of which I pass on the walk to work every morning. After several months of highly scientific tasting, there is nowhere else I get my daily cortado (and, when I'm feeling hedonistic, a ham and cheese croissant): the staff are lovely, the clientele is London in microcosm, the coffee is fantastic"
—GR

67 Exmouth Market,
Clerkenwell EC1R 4QL
briki.london • +44 2072788745
Open 7 days • £££

MARKETS

A trip to the local farmers' market is something of a weekend habit for many Londoners. Producers, artisans and entrepreneurial traders set up stall in temporarily deserted schoolyards, closed-off streets, car parks and even cemeteries. As a result, shoppers get access to a range of top quality treats such as free-range meats straight from the farm, fish landed that morning, a glut of seasonal vegetables, cheeses and charcuterie, jams and ferments, and baked goods and pastries. Hot food stalls are an increasingly significant element at most of these markets, but at the best of them fresh produce is still king.

London Farmers' Markets (LFM.org.uk) currently run around twenty different sites, notably Marylebone, Balham, Parliament Hill and Queens Park. Importantly, a strict criteria for their traders it that they grow or make the produce they sell, with seasonal and local produce vital too.

City & Country Farmers' Markets (wearecfm.com) play a similar role, curating well-supported markets in Herne Hill, Alexandra Palace, Oval and elsewhere. Other markets exist off their own ingenuity, maintaining an independent spirit and a particularly local character, such as Growing Communities in Stoke Newington (opposite).

Most produce markets are open only on a Saturday or Sunday, generally between 10am and 2pm. So early risers benefit from the cream of the produce. If your leisurely food shopping time extends through the week, though, then one dependable outlier is Borough Market (page 114), a bastion of the best fresh goods and artisan products from both Britain and around the world.

See also STREET FOOD (page 78)

97 Herne Hill Market

Recommended by Victoria Stewart

"Wandering through Herne Hill Market on a Sunday is lovely. It's situated along a pedestrianised street so there's seemingly space for everyone, and the produce is superb"—VS

Railton Road, Southwark SE24 0JN
weareccfm.com
Open Sunday • £££

98 Growing Communities Farmers' Market

Recommended by Ed Smith

"London's only fully organic market. This is a proper muddy roots, all shapes and sizes, stalls manned by the farmer sort of place. It is long-standing, popular with the local Stokey foodies, and an excellent place for a no-frills, country to the city, real food shop"—ES

St Paul's Church, Stoke Newington N16 7UY
growingcommunities.org
Open Saturday • £££

99 Brixton Market

Recommended by Victoria Stewart

"I love buying fresh fruit and veg from Brixton Market. I choose where I go depending on who's got what and when, but I like that it's always bright and misshapen produce, and that I can have a chat with the market sellers about how our days are going"—VS

Brixton Station Road, Brixton SW9 8PD
brixtonmarket.net
Open 7 days • £££

⑩ Broadway Market

Recommended by George Reynolds, Kar-Shing Tong

"It's just on the verge of becoming an in-the-know tourist hotspot, but for the time being Broadway is still just popular enough to make browsing the stalls a pleasurable activity. Start with a coffee from Climpson and Sons and proceed past the cheesemongers and greengrocers, the handicrafters and jamón-curers. Or stop for some excellent street food: a cheese and haggis toastie from Deeney's will cure any hangover, and a fried chicken sandwich from Butchies will practically give you one (in the best possible way). Get there now, before the hipsters ruin it forever"—*GR*

"The greatest traditional-style street food market in London"—*KST*

Broadway Market, Hackney E8 4QJ
broadwaymarket.co.uk
Open Saturday • £££

101 Borough Market

Recommended by Celia Brooks, Joanne Gould, Chloe Sachdev, Ed Smith, Kar-Shing Tong

"Nothing compares to the incredible range of top quality British produce as well as foods from all over Europe and the world. Top tip: Avoid Saturdays as it is unpleasantly overcrowded – Wednesday to Friday is best"—*CB*

"Borough Market every time. Bread Ahead for doughnuts, Brindisa for mini chorizo, and practically any stall for cheese"—*JG*

8 Southwark Street, Borough SE1 1TL
boroughmarket.org.uk • +44 2074071002
Closed Sunday • ££££

INGREDIENTS

To eat like a local is to not restrict yourself to restaurants and takeaways. Contrary to hype, very few Londoners eat out every night. Instead, they cook and entertain. This is, after all, a town that's fostered a thousand supper clubs, "underground" restaurants and enthusiastic amateurs who turn street food hobbies into all-conquering chains.

If there's one thing London's population has learnt from countless food TV shows, cookery books and restaurant openings, it's that produce is key; if you start with the good stuff, there's very little more that needs doing. It follows that many locals relish quality produce vendors – be they butchers, cheesemongers, bakers, grocers, fishmongers or delicatessens covering all of those things and more.

Some shops are historic; an essential visit for foodies wishing to understand a little more about London's food heritage and culture. The likes of Neal's Yard Dairy (page 122) and Lina Stores (opposite) fall into this category.

Others are curators of quality, yes, but they err towards functional and modest too. It's the ingredients they sell that do the talking, not a fancy display unit, cookbook or PR strategy. These are shrines to whole carcass butchery; stiff as a board, day-boat caught fish; vegetables and fruits that have been harvested at their seasonal peak; and artisanal produce sourced from the city it's sold in.

Check your kitchen has a sharp knife and working oven, then take some bags, go shopping and build up an appetite.

102 Lina Stores

Recommended by Joanne Gould

"For the most authentic and hard to find pasta, meats and other Italian goodies" —*JG*

A family-run Italian delicatessen in the heart of Soho, founded over 70 years ago. Initially a supplier to the (then) many Italian immigrant restaurants in the area, it's now a friendly source of the best Italian cured meats, pasta, antipasti and sweet treats for central London's workers and visitors alike. There are fresh sandwiches, hot meals and coffee to go too.

18 Brewer Street, Soho W1F 0SH
linastores.co.uk • +44 2074376482
Open 7 days • ££££

103 The Hampstead Butcher & Providore

Recommended by Joanne Gould

"Amazing, well-sourced meat, interesting groceries, burrata, bone marrow, cheese... I could go on. And they can get you almost anything if you ask ahead of time"—*JG*

56 Rosslyn Hill, Hampstead NW3 1ND
(see website for other locations)
hampsteadbutcher.com
+44 2077949210
Open 7 days • ££££

104 The Quality Chop Shop

Recommended by Catherine & Gavin Hanly, George Reynolds

"Shaun Searley's gaff next door is – for good reason – celebrated as one of the best Modern British restaurants in the city; his shop does a similar job of presenting excellent ingredients in their most flattering light. There is an on-site butcher; there are cans of Navarrico pulses and tins of Ortiz anchovies. There is also a fridge filled with some of Searley's greatest hits: the comforting Hereford mince; the outrageous confit potatoes. Add a loaf of house sourdough and you've got an instant, excellent, dinner party (or, in my case, a very indulgent midweek supper)"—*GR*

88–94 Farringdon Road, Clerkenwell EC1R 3EA
shop.thequalitychophouse.com • +44 2034906228
Open 7 days • ££££

105 Neal's Yard Dairy

Recommended by Ed Smith

"They've a few shops, including the original in Covent Garden, but for a near-spiritual cheese moment, head to Neal's Yard Dairy's Cathedral-like site on the edge of Borough Market. The curators and promoters of Britain's brilliant artisan cheese movement provide a first-class shopping experience – as your personal server takes you through a full-on sampling session while you make up your mind. A brilliant way to stock up all year round, but absolutely essential at Christmastime"—ES

6 Park Street, Borough Market SE1 9AB
(see website for other locations)
nealsyarddairy.co.uk • +44 2073670799
Closed Sunday • £££

106 Japan Centre

Recommended by Liz & Max Haarala Hamilton

"Great for savoury snacks, from sashimi to seaweed, and crazy Japanese biscuits and sweets"—L&MHH

A real destination for foodies looking for their fix of Japanese cuisine. The Japan Store's site near Leicester Square is a food court full of groceries, larder goods and sashimi-grade fish, as well as a central dine-in courtyard. An exotic and authentic resource.

35B Panton Street, St James's SW1Y 4EA
(see website for other locations)
japancentre.com • +44 2034051246
Open 7 days • £££

107 ## Moen & Sons

Recommended by Victoria Stewart

"I buy meat from Moen & Sons in Clapham, because I can trust the quality. The butchers know their stuff and are lovely to chat to!"—*VS*

24 The Pavement, Clapham Common SW4 0JA
moen.co.uk • +44 2076221624
Closed Sunday • ££££

108 ## Panzer's Deli & Grocery

Recommended by Chloe Sachdev

"Has some of the best produce in London. Their bagels and salmon are superlative"—*CS*

13–19 Circus Road, St John's Wood NW8 6PB
panzers.co.uk • +44 2077228162
Open 7 days • ££££

If you are charged with buying London-themed gifts for foodie friends, consider the many edible items that are made in London. The city's artisanal producer scene grows from strength to strength – you'll find locally made cheeses, cured meats, chocolates, jams, pickles and preserves, all perfectly packaged for present giving, and many of them with long enough legs to travel without refrigeration (provided you're disciplined enough to not tuck in).

Some producers sell direct from farmers' markets (page 110), while others have found their way to the shelves of independent delicatessens, which tend to be found on bijou streets in neighbourhoods such as Hackney, Islington, Notting Hill, Peckham and Dulwich. Sourced Market (page 126), who have a number of different outlets in prime, central spots near transport hubs, are an excellent curator of contemporary London produce.

If your luggage allowance permits it, consider some locally brewed or distilled alcohol. There are upwards of 70 London craft breweries, and some fantastic gin distilleries too (look out for Sipsmith, Jensen's, and the East London Liquor Company, page 128). These drinks tend to be stocked by independent wine and bottle shops, rather than supermarkets. As with the delicatessens, these need to be sought out and tend to be in relatively affluent or up-and-coming neighbourhoods.

For more traditionally British edible gifts, there's always the famous Fortnum & Mason food hall on Piccadilly (opposite). The Queen's grocers and provision merchants stocks fabulously packaged sweet treats, savoury delights, condiments, exotic teas and more, over multiple, majestic and history-steeped floors.

109 # Selfridges Food Hall

Recommended by Chloe Sachdev

"Always has great selection of everything from chocolates to wine"—*CS*

Crammed full of both glitzy international and artisanal British treats, Selfridges Food Hall provides a multitude of options for food and drink gifts, as well as fresh groceries, food to go, and a selection of informal restaurant concessions.

400 Oxford Street, Marylebone W1A 1AB
selfridges.com • +44 1133698040
Open 7 days • ££££

110 # Fortnum & Mason

Recommended by Kar-Shing Tong

"Fortnum & Mason is an oldie but very much a goodie. When in need of edible gifts, I always manage to find something in here which is perfect"—*KST*

Set over five floors, this is a veritable cornucopia of treats – from the finest teas, cakes and toffees in gift tins, to acclaimed wicker hampers. Oak panelled lifts, grand staircase and doormen in top hats complete the very British experience.

181 Piccadilly, St James's W1A 1ER
(see website for other locations)
fortnumandmason.com • +44 2077348040
Open 7 days • ££££

111 # Yauatcha

Recommended by Catherine & Gavin Hanly

"Macarons from Yauatcha come in the most beautifully presented box – and they're always doing some really interesting seasonal flavours"—*C&GH*

Though principally a contemporary dim sum restaurant serving the finest dumplings, Yauatcha's desserts, sweet macarons and extensive tea selection are also available gift wrapped to go.

15–17 Broadwick Street, Soho W1F 0DL
(see website for other locations)
yauatcha.com • +44 2074948888
Open 7 days • ££££

SOURCED
MARKET
We are an independent retailer & our aim is to carefully source our produce from the best of Britain's small, artisan producers
Bakery
Coffee
Grocery
Wine & Beer
Kitchen Deli
Juice Bar
Delicatessen
SOURCED
SOURCED
MARKET
HANGRY

112 Sourced Market

Recommended by George Reynolds, Ed Smith, Victoria Stewart, Kar-Shing Tong

"Whenever I take the train to visit my parents I leave an extra few minutes to rifle through the shelves at Sourced Market in search of a present (that sometimes, unfortunately, becomes a picnic on board). Particular highlights have included high-grade chorizo, an armful of practically liquid French cheese and Torres' insanely addictive black truffle crisps (buy an extra bag to pimp your train ride)"—*GR*

St Pancras International, King's Cross N1C 4QP
(see website for other locations)
sourcedmarket.com • +44 2078339352
Open 7 days • ££££

⑬ East London Liquor Company

Recommended by Ed Smith

"I like gifts that have a story behind them, and also ones that are drinkable, which makes the East London Liquor Company one of my favourite places to pick up a bottle to pass on. They distil excellent gin and rum near Victoria Park in east London, and are waiting on their first batch of whisky. You can buy from a shop at their distillery, and also their stall in Borough Market"—*ES*

Unit GF1, 221 Grove Road,
Hackney E3 5SN
(see website for stockists)
eastlondonliquorcompany.com
Open 7 days • ££££

RECIPES

Kedgeree

Welsh Rarebit

Homemade Beans on Toast

Dressed Chicken Livers

Chicken & Leek Pie

Victoria Sponge

Pear & Sherry Trifle

Pimm's Cup

Gin Gimlet

Kedgeree

A hearty Anglo-Indian breakfast dish made with rice, smoked fish and hard-boiled eggs.

Serves 2

80g basmati rice

150g smoked haddock

150ml milk

1 bay leaf

½ tbsp vegetable oil

½ onion, finely chopped

½ tbsp curry powder

2 eggs, hard-boiled, peeled and cut into quarters

Small handful of fresh parsley, chopped

Small handful of fresh coriander, chopped

Sea salt and freshly ground black pepper

Lemon wedges, to serve

Cook the rice according to the packet instructions and set aside.

Poach the smoked haddock in the milk with the bay leaf for 10 minutes, or until the haddock is fully opaque and starting to flake apart. Drain, reserving about a third of the poaching liquid, and put the haddock to one side to cool.

Heat the oil in a frying pan over a medium heat and sauté the chopped onion until soft and translucent. Add the curry powder and stir through.

Flake the fish into large chunks and add to the pan along with the cooked rice and reserved poaching liquid. Stir gently and take off the heat once the rice is warmed through. Season to taste (bearing in mind that smoked haddock is typically quite salty).

Top with the quartered eggs, parsley and coriander and serve with a few lemon wedges.

Welsh Rarebit

A souped-up version of cheese on toast that's well worth the extra effort. This comforting traditional British savoury can now be found on many a London menu.

Serves 2 as a snack

30g butter

30g plain flour

150ml milk or beer

150g Cheddar, grated

1 tsp English mustard

A good dash of Worcestershire sauce

2 thick slices of best quality bread

Freshly ground black pepper

Preheat the grill to medium-high.

Melt the butter in a small pan over a medium heat and add the flour to make a roux. Cook, stirring constantly, for a couple of minutes, until the mixture turns slightly golden.

Add the milk or beer, a little at a time, stirring well to incorporate. Add the grated Cheddar and continue to stir until melted.

Remove from the heat, stir in the mustard and Worcestershire sauce and season with black pepper.

Toast the bread on both sides before smoothing on the cheesy mixture. Grill for about 5 minutes until bubbling and golden.

Homemade Beans on Toast

"Baked beans" are a British staple, whether eaten simply on toast, with a jacket potato or as part of the ubiquitous fry up. The homemade version is just as comforting, and far more delicious.

Serves 2

Small knob of butter, plus extra for the toast

1 small onion, finely chopped

2 tbsp tomato purée

400g tin cannellini beans

A good splash of Worcestershire sauce

Pinch of sugar

4 thick slices of granary bread

Sea salt and freshly ground black pepper

Melt the butter in a small pan over a low-medium heat. Add the onion and a pinch of salt and sauté for 5–10 minutes, until soft and translucent.

Add the tomato purée and stir for a minute. Add the cannellini beans, liquid and all, and bring to the boil. Simmer for 5 minutes before adding the Worcestershire sauce and a pinch of sugar. Season to taste.

Toast the bread and spread over a little butter. Top with the beans and their sauce. Add an extra grind of black pepper and serve immediately.

Dressed Chicken Livers

After years of being shunned, offal is having a real revival in modern British cuisine. Cooked well and given a simple treatment, these chicken livers make a satisfying lunch. Serve with a green salad and plenty of crusty bread.

Serves 2

30g butter

A splash of olive oil

400g very fresh chicken livers

Juice of 1 lemon

1 heaped tbsp capers, roughly chopped

Handful of fresh parsley, finely chopped

Sea salt and freshly ground black pepper

Melt the butter and olive oil in a wide frying pan over a medium-high heat. Once the butter is bubbling, add the chicken livers in a single layer. Fry for 2–3 minutes on each side, until burnished and brown on the outside but still slightly pink on the inside.

Take off the heat before adding the lemon juice, capers and parsley to the pan. Stir through, coating the livers in the warm dressing. Season to taste and serve immediately.

Chicken & Leek Pie

A good pie is one of the things the Brits do best and is a staple on every pub menu. Serve this flaky number with steamed seasonal veg in the summer, and hearty mashed potato in the winter.

Serves 4–6

30g butter

3–4 fresh thyme sprigs

1.5kg leeks, trimmed and thinly sliced into rounds

2 tbsp plain flour

1 litre chicken stock

100ml single cream

750g cooked chicken breast or thigh, shredded

320g sheet puff pastry

Beaten egg, to glaze

Sea salt and freshly ground black pepper

Preheat the oven to 220°C.

Melt the butter in a large pan over a medium heat. Add the thyme and leeks and stir until coated with butter. Turn the heat to low, add a generous pinch of salt and cover with a tight-fitting lid. Leave the leeks to sweat for about 30 minutes, stirring occasionally. They will release plenty of moisture as they cook down, creating a delicious base for your pie.

Once the leeks have had 30 minutes, tip in the flour and cook over a medium heat, stirring constantly, for about 5 minutes. Once the leeks are starting to brown at the edges, pour in the stock and bring to the boil. Leave to simmer over a low heat for 10 minutes, until the sauce has thickened slightly. Remove from the heat and stir in the cream and the shredded chicken. Season to taste.

Strain the contents of the pan through a sieve over a large bowl to collect all the saucy gravy. Return the gravy to the pan and set aside, ready to reheat when the pie is done. Tip the drained leeks and chicken into a shallow ovenproof dish, about 20 x 25cm, and top with the pastry sheet, tucking in any overlapping edges. Cut a cross in the middle of the pastry to allow steam to escape and brush all over with beaten egg.

Bake in the oven for 35 minutes, until the pastry is golden. Serve with the reheated gravy.

Victoria Sponge

The quintessential British cake, so good that it's named after royalty.
Light, fluffy and perfect with a cup of milky English breakfast tea.

For the sponge

200g butter, at room temperature

200g caster sugar

4 eggs

2 tsp vanilla extract

200g plain flour

2 tsp baking powder

1–2 tbsp milk (optional)

For the filling

140g icing sugar

100g butter, at room temperature

150g strawberry jam

Grease and line two shallow 20cm cake tins and preheat the oven to 180°C.

To make the sponge, cream the butter and sugar with a wooden spoon. Beat in the eggs, one at a time, before adding the vanilla extract. Sift in the plain flour and baking powder, adding a little milk if the mixture is too thick to stir.

Smooth half the cake mix into each of your prepared tins. Bake in the oven for about 20 minutes; the cakes are done when a knife or skewer poked into the centre of the cake comes out clean.

For the filling, sift the icing sugar into a large bowl and beat in the butter until smooth. Once the cakes have cooled, turn them out and spread one half with the buttercream and dollop on the jam. Sandwich the two cakes together and serve.

Pear & Sherry Trifle

Trifle is something of an institution in Britain and can often be found (in refined form) on the menus of top modern British restaurants across London. It has a lot to offer, with fruit, sponge, custard and cream combining to create a delicious dessert perfect for rounding off any meal.

Serves 6

500g pears

1 tbsp caster sugar

12 amaretti biscuits

150ml sherry

200ml whipping cream

20g flaked almonds, toasted

For the custard

2 large egg yolks

2 tbsp caster sugar, plus extra to sprinkle

2 tbsp cornflour

400ml milk

200ml single cream

Peel and core the pears and cut into 1cm wedges. Put in a pan with the sugar and 2 tablespoons water. Simmer for 5–10 minutes, until the pears still hold their shape but can easily be pierced with a knife. Take off the heat and set aside.

For the custard, whisk together the egg yolks, caster sugar and cornflour in a large bowl. Heat the milk and single cream in a pan until almost, but not quite, boiling. Slowly pour the hot liquid over the egg yolk mixture, whisking constantly to prevent curdling. Transfer the contents of the bowl back into the pan and stir over a medium-high heat until the mixture just comes to the boil and thickens. Take off the heat and sprinkle with caster sugar (to prevent a skin from forming) before setting aside to cool.

Gently crush the amaretti biscuits with your hands and arrange in the base of a large glass bowl. Place the poached pears on top and evenly pour over the sherry. Spoon the custard over the pears and spread to create an even layer. Whip the cream to soft peaks and dollop over the custard. Chill for at least an hour and sprinkle with the toasted almonds before serving.

Pimm's Cup

The ultimate summer cocktail, to be found in beer gardens across the city the very moment the sun comes out. Turn it into a "Pimm's Royale" by substituting the lemonade with sparkling white wine.

Serves 4

A handful of strawberries, halved

¼ cucumber, thickly sliced into half-moons

1 orange, cut into slim wedges

A couple of mint sprigs

200ml Pimm's

600ml lemonade, chilled

Put plenty of ice cubes and a few pieces of strawberry, cucumber, orange and mint in each of the four glasses.

Fill a pitcher with ice and load in the rest of the garnishes. Pour in the Pimm's and top up with the lemonade. Stir and serve immediately.

Gin Gimlet

Gin has long been a staple of the London drinking scene and is currently enjoying a huge revival. Most commonly drunk simply with tonic and a slice of lemon or lime, there are plenty of cocktails to be enjoyed. The gimlet is simple and classic and has its origins in the navy, where it was drunk by sailors to stave off scurvy.

Mix three parts gin with one part Rose's Lime Cordial in a glass filled with ice. Strain into a chilled cocktail glass and garnish with a thin slice of lime.

INDEX **A TO Z**

INDEX **BY LOCAL**

BLOOMSBURY PUBLISHING
Bloomsbury Publishing Plc
50 Bedford Square, London WC1B 3DP

BLOOMSBURY, BLOOMSBURY PUBLISHING and the Diana logo
are trademarks of Bloomsbury Publishing Plc

First published in Great Britain 2018

A catalogue record for this book is available from the British Library

ISBN: 978-1-4088-9323-4

2 4 6 8 10 9 7 5 3 1

Series Editor: Lena Hall
Contributing Writer: Ed Smith
Cover Designer: Greg Heinimann
Designer: Julyan Bayes
Photographer: Ola O. Smit
Production Controller: Arlene Alexander

Printed and bound in China by RR Donnelley Asia Printing Solutions Ltd.

Bloomsbury Publishing Plc makes every effort to ensure that the papers used in the manufacture
of our books are natural, recyclable products made from wood grown in well-managed forests.
Our manufacturing processes conform to the environmental regulations of the country of origin

To find out more about our authors and books visit
www.bloomsbury.com and sign up for our newsletters

BREAKFAST

1. St John Bread and Wine — H6
2. Granger & Co. — D4
3. Hawksmoor — D7
4. The Wolseley — C7
5. Royal China Club — B6
6. Duck and Waffle — G6
7. Café Z Bar — H1

CLASSIC LONDON

8. Sweetings — G7
9. Goddards at Greenwich — J8
10. Maria's Market Café — G8
11. Silva's — D6
12. Beigel Bake — H5
13. Poppie's — H6
14. The Golden Hind — B6

BRITISH

15. St John Bar and Restaurant — F6
16. Rules — D7
17. Holborn Dining Room — E6
18. Simpson's in the Strand — E7
19. The Clove Club — H5
20. Clipstone — C6
21. Elliot's — G7
22. Lyle's — H5

PUB KITCHEN

23. The Eagle — E5
24. The Canton Arms — D8
25. The Camberwell Arms — G8
26. The Drapers Arms — E3
27. Marksman — H4

SUNDAY ROAST

28. Blacklock — C7
29. The Windsor Castle — I2
30. The Adam & Eve — J2
31. The Bull & Gate — C2
32. The Bull & Last — B1

SMALL PLATES

33. The Palomar — D7
34. Bocca di Lupo — D7
35. Ceviche — G5
36. Hopscotch — H5
37. Barrafina — D6
38. Kiln — C7
39. Naughty Piglets — E8
40. Casita Andina — D7

CURRY

41. DUM Biryani House — C6
42. Gunpowder — H6
43. Kricket — C7
44. Dishoom — H5
45. Gymkhana — C7
46. Jamavar — B7
47. Madame D — H6

NOODLES

48. Kanada-Ya — D6
49. Koya Bar — D6
50. Salvation in Noodles — G2
51. Baozi Inn — D7
52. Mien Tay — H4

CHINESE

53. Bao — D6
54. Hunan — B8
55. Silk Road — G8
56. Mamalan — H5
57. XU — D7
58. Chilli Cool — D5
59. Shikumen — A7
60. Leong's Legend — D7

MANGAL

61. Black Axe Mangal — F2
62. Testi — H1
63. Antepliler — F1
64. Gökyüzü — F1
65. Likya — A1

STREET FOOD

66. Maltby Street Market — H8
67. Leather Lane Market — E6
68. Druid Street Market — H8
69. Dinerama — H5
70. KERB — various

ICE CREAM

71. Gelateria 3Bis — G8
72. Nonna's Gelato — various
73. Chin Chin Labs — C3
74. Gelupo — D7
75. Four Winters — C7

COCKTAILS

76. Sager + Wilde — I5
77. Dukes Bar — C8
78. Luca Bar — F5
79. Claridge's — B7
80. Nightjar — G5
81. Every Cloud — I2

WINE BARS

82. The Remedy — C5
83. 40 Maltby Street — H8
84. Gordon's Wine Bar — D7
85. P. Franco — J2
86. Noble Rot — E5

PUBS

87. The Southampton Arms — C1
88. The Barrowboy & Banker — G7
89. The Lamb — E5
90. Chesham Arms — J2

COFFEE

91. Allpress — H2
92. Monmouth — G8
93. Grind — G5
94. Origin — G5
95. Prufrock — E6
96. Briki — E5

MARKETS

97. Herne Hill Market — F8
98. Growing Communities — H1
99. Brixton Market — E8
100. Broadway Market — I4
101. Borough Market — G8

INGREDIENTS

102. Lina Stores — C7
103. The Hampstead Butcher — A1
104. The Quality Chop Shop — E5
105. Neal's Yard Dairy — G8
106. Japan Centre — D7
107. Moen & Sons — C8
108. Panzer's Deli & Grocery — A4

PRESENTS

109. Selfridges Food Hall — B6
110. Fortnum & Mason — C7
111. Yauatcha — C6
112. Sourced Market — D4
113. East London Liquor — J4